Herstellung und Verlag:
BoD - Books on Demand, Norderstedt

ISBN 978-3-8482-2147-9

Layout: Stephan Pegels • www.step-design.com

From Dorsten to Chicago

**Lectures and contributions
of the Eisendrath Family Reunion 2010
in Dorsten/Germany**

Edited by Elisabeth Cosanne-Schulte-Huxel
Published by the Jewish Museum of Westphalia

Dorsten 2012
Books on Demand

Content

Elisabeth Cosanne-Schulte-Huxel
Foreword

"I set off on my journey to Dorsten with many questions on the sense of such a meeting but it was a real discovery for me. It has given part of my life more depth and a new look at interaction, for example with my father," wrote Henri Eisendrath from Belgium in August 2010.

We had the same reservations when we started our planning. Was it a mad idea to invite the descendants of a family to Dorsten who had left for the "New World", especially Chicago, some 150 years ago? But I can say that for all those involved, be they hosts or guests, it was an interesting and successful venture.

We have been looking at the Eisendrath family history for some years. In 1982 we started our research and in the archives we found a great deal of information on life here in Dorsten and emigration to Chicago. In 1988 I traveled to the U.S. and made the first contact with Joseph Eisendrath from Chicago and Clem and Alyne Bonnell from Milford, N.J. The information they supplied was used in the book "Juden in Dorsten und in der Herrlichkeit Lembeck" published in 1989.

Clem Bonnell has carried out extensive genealogical research on the Eisendrath family. Without all this impressive work, a lot of what we know about the family would not have been possible. We would like to use this opportunity to express our sincere thanks to Clem Bonnell for all his work. Stefan Eisendrath from Lennik, Belgium took over the family research. He documented this very well at the family reunion in Dorsten. All the participants were able to find themselves in extensive family trees, a very impressive achievement. (For technical reasons we are unfortunately not able to reproduce the genealogy in the book.)

In the past 20 years many Eisendraths – both young and old – have traveled "back to the roots" to Dorsten. In 2010 some Eisendraths were in Dorsten for the second time. Again and again the meetings have enriched our archive material with new photos and documents. And thus the website "www.eisendrath-stories.net" has been developed with lots of stories about the family.

In an amusing speech at the reunion, Charles Eisendrath, who had already been to Dorsten in 1998, described how "between Boston and Moscow" he had discovered this remarkable place and its special museum. In 2001, together with other members of the family, he donated money through the Council of Michigan Foundation for the restoration of the Eisendrath graves at the Jewish cemetery in Dorsten.

Family meetings played a big role in the tradition of the Eisendraths. It did not always have to be a big occasion such as, for example, Eva Eisendrath's wedding attended by over 200 guests. On the contrary, monthly cousins' meetings in Chicago with over 50 people were not unusual. Some 80 years ago Dina Wolf Heymansohn said the following:

"Good friends all, I give you greeting,
At this merry cousins' meeting,
Where we find it most amusing
To be feasting here and shmoosing
Where it's natural that I rejoice
And that I give my feelings voice,
In welcome to you friends so dear
Who joyfully have gathered here
To show that we together hold,
Just like the Eisendraths of old.
To meet our cousins and the rest
They live way north, south, east and west.
Therefore don't know of any reason
Why we won't have a busy season
Of cousins' parties just like this,
Where not one member we should miss.
These monthly gatherings that we have,
We eat, we play, we talk and we laugh."

And that was how we planned the family reunion. There were meetings with members of the Museum Association, with the Mayor of Dorsten, with Count von Merveldt and many others, talks, discussions, tours of the town, a visit to the cemetery, a barbecue and lots of conversations. In his letter of 5 April 2011, Charles Eisendrath put it as follows: "I put 'reunion' in quotation marks because in English this signals that the meaning in a particular context is not the same as in dictionary definition. What you gave all of us was far more than a reunion. It was really a combination of an introduction to Germany, to Westphalia, to Dorsten, to each other, to you and the Museum, all in the context of an academic conference, complete with exhibitions, scholarly research papers and directed discussions. You even invented a new kind of academic conference, one in which the subject matter (the Eisendraths) were also the students. I have been a professor for 30 years but found this completely novel."

We had written to around 150 family members in the U.S. and Belgium. In July 2010, 50 people between 5 and 89 years of age said they were coming to the first reunion in Dorsten. We were very surprised at the great number of responses. Some of them came a really long way – from San Francisco, Illinois, Boston, Michigan, New York, Wisconsin, Los Angeles, Chicago, Washington D.C., California, Maryland and from Belgium to discover their family roots in Dorsten and the surrounding area. We had planned and prepared a lot but there were also some spontaneous improvisations, e.g. a visit to a school or a swimming pool with the children. For us it was quite a venture. But we are very grateful that we had excellent helpers. And everybody agreed: "We had great fun with the Eisendraths."

The many thank-you letters and mails we received convinced us, too. They confirm that we did the right thing with this unique and wonderful experiment. As an example, I would like to mention Edith Silberstein: "I often think back to the few days in Dorsten. You gave me and my family very much."

There's a German saying which goes: "You meet everybody twice in life … and that may well be sooner than you think". Please keep in touch with Dorsten and your 'new' family members.

Impressions

Norbert Reichling

 # An introduction to the Jewish Museum of Westphalia
Including some remarks on German Memorial Culture

An extraordinary week of meetings, excursions and discussions in summer 2010 is what we are recalling with this collection of papers and reports. The museum team was very surprised and also very happy that so many Eisendraths were brave enough to follow our invitation. They came with open-minded attitudes and in that week they contributed to an experience that both they and we were privileged to enjoy: trackbacking on a history in which Dorsten's past and their family roots are entwined.

The Eisendrath family and its history have been accompanying us since the very beginning of our institution. Research on this special family history formed part of the pioneering research carried out by a small group of Dorsten citizens in the 1980s. But I will get back to this point later.

This foreword would like to give the readers some basic facts about our museum and also some information on the everyday tasks we perform here. But at first a few words to depict the role of our small museum within the larger framework of memorial culture in Germany.

A long way...

"Coming to terms with the past" after WW II is a long and complicated story in Germany, full of mistake, scandals – and it is a history of a minority of dedicated individuals in the legal system, in schools, in politics, at memorial sites; a few survivors, of course, belonged to these activists, too. (To make a complicated chapter a little clearer, we are not looking on the development in East Germany).

It is well known that for a long time talking about Nazi history, about Nazi crimes and the extermination of European Jewry was not very popular in Germany. We are therefore looking back to a long period of silence, of sugarcoating the past, of playing down the mass murder of the years between 1933 and 1945. In this first postwar period only an extremely small percentage of the perpetrators were prosecuted and sentenced by German law courts. It was a time when it was even difficult to speak about the "other Germans" – those who resisted the terrorist regime. These brave people were often seen as "traitors" – at least until the end of the fifties, sometimes even longer.

The critical confrontation with the real history of the Holocaust – as far as large sections of our society are concerned – started at the beginning of the sixties: with some Nazis prosecuted for their crimes (the Auschwitz trial in Frankfurt for example), with a few memorial institutions and a handful of activists. And this confrontation began very slowly: New subjects were taught in schools, new generations of teachers had to be trained etc. Only three stages of the further development are summarized below – and that is, of course, a rather simplified sketch.

The 1980s
As the years passed, new generations grew up with completely different attitudes to those of the Nazi perpetrators. These generations developed the ability to learn and talk about this cruel reality. A new phenomenon of the 1980s should be mentioned here: dedicated laymen who formed so called "history workshops"; sometimes they labelled themselves "barefoot historians". Their aim was to examine more closely how the general history taught in the educational institutions and in the history books had looked in their towns, in their streets, at the company next door. Nearly every West German town was affected by these ambitions of "alternative" bottom-up historiography. Such activities produced harsh controversies between older and younger generations in Germany – the older ones often underlining that they also suffered hardship as a result of the war.

A crucial step for public debate was the speech delivered by Richard von Weizsäcker in May 1985 on the occasion of the 40th anniversary of the end of World War II on 8 May 1945. This president – the son of a man involved in Nazi foreign policy – finally dared to emphasize that all groups of Nazi victims have a right to be honored (including Communists, slave laborers, homosexuals, the so called "anti-social", gypsies etc.). That was a new tone in Germany, and it clearly demonstrated that perspectives were changing.

Another dispute of the 1980s needs to be noted: the so-called "historians' dispute": some conservative historians tried to teach us that the Nazis were not as criminal as the Bolsheviks, that their crimes had been a more or less exaggerated reaction to Communist threats. Months of intense debate followed (in newspapers, on TV, with series of books and conferences). The result was the opposite to what had been intended: since then we have had a broadly based consensus that the planned industrial murder of European Jewry should be seen as the center of what the Nazis did – and not their anti-Bolshevism, their nationalism, their war. And this consensus includes the point that this "rupture of civilization" by state crimes has been shown to be the negative starting point of a new and ethic based policy in Germany after 1945 (whatever this means in detail...).

One problem of such an approach might be seen in a certain bias of identification with the Jewish victims. And it also became a new source of Jewish-Christian reconciliation activities. This can, of course, go too far: that is the case when people ignore the personal roots in a society of perpetrators and bystanders, if they are not interested enough in the details, e.g. in the involvement of their forefathers in the crimes.

German Reunification
The fall of the Berlin Wall and of the second German state, the German Democratic Republic (GDR), had a major impact on our questions: the simplified anti-fascist ideology of the Communists ruling that other German state was one of the foundations of their power – and after 1990 it lost all credibility. The inevitable task of comparing dictatorships emerged from the reunification: it became necessary also because of the "double history" of some places like Buchenwald or Sachsenhausen – Nazi concentration camps and, in the years after 1945, detention camps of the Soviets. After WW II a large number of (minor) Nazis and people from the anti-Soviet resistance (lots of them democrats, even socialists)

were interned in these places. Much irritation has arisen from these discussions up to today – firstly among the victims of the Nazis who fear that the fate of the Nazis interned might be compared to the terrible suffering that they, the victims, were subjected to, but also among those who resisted Communist dictatorship and were tortured by some of the Communists previously oppressed by the Nazis.

What was the way out of this dilemma? New research and new exhibitions (not only in eastern Germany, but in the whole republic!) have emerged from these discussions. Exhibitions are becoming less pathetic and more complicated – what we find now in these memorials are rather ambitious messages. They speak about ambivalences and a wide range of moral options during the Nazi years. To summarize what they teach: stop binary thinking!

One effect of these difficulties in the political field has been that the major camp memorials also in western Germany (for example Dachau, Bergen-Belsen, Neuengamme) are now finally seen as a public task: there is a federal responsibility and there have been public grants for them since the end of the 1990s (as in the former GDR).

The situation today
The intention of the international debates on Holocaust and Holocaust education following the international Stockholm conference of 2000 has been to establish a sort of universal lesson from the Holocaust, the effort to gain a new global impulse for human rights education from this experience. Many experts ask: is this sort of global message perhaps too abstract? One can see the danger of unhistorical thinking, of simplified messages for everybody in the world. We still believe in the effects of knowledge, of knowledge of distinct historical situations. "Only knowledge?" we are sometimes asked, and we answer: "It is possible to promote empathy by knowledge."

But we still need some sort of new approach because as a result of immigration Germany is becoming more multiethnic – a salad bowl of identities in every classroom, historical experiences from all over the world, even national myths which have gained new vitality after 1989.

All perspectives should be represented: those of the victims, of perpetrators, of bystanders, and those of helpers. The forgotten rescuers have been rediscovered within the last 10 years, the "Righteous" as Yad Vashem in Israel calls them. A new memorial has, for example, been established in Berlin for Otto Weidt, a kind of Schindler on an smaller scale. Such a place is not important in the sense of "How well the Germans did", but it has the effect of raising new questions of individual responsibility. Its message is "People could do something even during those years!" This will not be the end of the debate about the question: who is worthy of remembrance, where and how? A memorial for the murdered homosexuals has followed the Holocaust memorial in Berlin, one for the gypsies will be added – and so on...

Jewish Museums

Jewish Museums are a special case within this memorial landscape in Germany. Many of the Jewish museums have been established since the 1990s. The collections in Berlin (since 2001) and in Munich (opened in 2007) have become well-known, also because of their outstanding architecture. The Frankfurt Jewish Museum should be highlighted too, as the earliest institution founded in 1988. These larger institutions are public museums, run by the Federal Republic (as in Berlin) or by rather wealthy cities.

Many small museums have been established in former synagogues – a lot of them suffered in the 'Kristallnacht' pogroms of 1938, especially in southern Germany. Of course, all these museums were developed in the knowledge of what happened in the Holocaust: the extermination of German Jewry as existed before, the presence of very small Jewish communities, and everyone was aware that these institutions had to be established, promoted and supported by non-Jews. This fundamental situation has changed slightly within the last decade: Jewish communities have been strengthened by immigration from the former Soviet Union, and we now also have a number of young Jewish people who are capable of running museums and working on excellent exhibitions.

The Jewish Museum in Dorsten
Finally some words about the museum in Dorsten. The Jewish Museum of Westphalia is a small museum – playing in the second league, as we sometimes joke. In our exhibitions we focus on regional history.

We display examples of how Jews lived in Westphalia before, during and after the Holocaust. It should be mentioned that the history of our museum is a rather typical story: just like our museum, most of the smaller museums and memorials were started by grassroots activities.

The plan to form such a documentation centre and the association behind it grew from the research activities of a small group of volunteers – called "Dorsten under the Swastika". This group was part of the alternative "history movement" mentioned before – citizens concerned about some forgotten issues, especially the history of the Jewish communities. By and by the group activists extended their perspectives, had a look at the 19th century, at the beginning of the rights for Jews to settle in Westphalia, at the stories of Jewish families in Dorsten like the Eisendraths, the Reifeisens or the Perlsteins. Supported by many citizens and local authorities we were gradually able to develop this collection and exhibition, beginning in 1992. The new museum building, where the permanent exhibition is now presented, was added in 2001 with the help of our federal state of North-Rhine-Westphalia.

A few words on our mission: the principal message of this museum is the remembrance of a rich German-Jewish history – a history of neighborliness, of mutual enrichment of both Jewish and non-Jewish Germans. We present some fundamental information on Jewish life, e.g., the meaning of things like the Torah, Synagogue, Shabbat, Bar Mitzvah and other festivals. These aspects are rather important for both the old and young in Germany. There are not many Jews living here and as the few who are here live a rather sheltered, discreet manner of being Jewish, knowledge of these traditions is generally very limited. In addition, it should be mentioned that more than 90 % of the members of the Jewish community are actually immigrants from the former Soviet Union who came here within the last 20 years. For this reason they are not able to say anything about German-Jewish history – a role we have to fill for a while.

The second section of our exhibition displays 14 biographies from the Middle Ages up to today: examples of the struggle for emancipation and equal political rights, from the "Golden Age" of German Jewry during the Weimar Republic after 1919 and, last but not least, a number of biographies of people who suffered persecution in the Shoah.

But it should be stressed out that we do not want to be a Holocaust museum. I can quote here from a report by Charles Eisendrath, written in 1999, based on a meeting with Sister Johanna Eichmann, my predecessor as director of this museum and today our Honorary President: "Here, in Holocaust heartland, the creator of one of the Jewish outposts volunteered that she would not permit her center to emphasize how Germany's Jews had been destroyed. Instead, it emphasized how they had lived". Though, of course, many of our issues are influenced by the Holocaust, despite the fact that our address is in Julius-Ambrunn-Strasse, named after the last speaker of the Jewish Community in Dorsten before deportations began, this is still a guideline of our team.

And, of course, one of our tasks is to work against anti-Semitism – the spread of knowledge about Jewry and Judaism does not help in all cases but it is sometimes useful in fighting this never-ending poison which remains a problem in all European societies.

Running a Jewish museum can be complicated for non-Jews – it is necessary to keep a certain distance: we need and we want to reflect the diversity of Jewish life. It would be a serious mistake if we depicted Jewish life, Jewish identities and Jewish culture as something clear, something uniform, stable for centuries. The first aim of the exhibitions, lectures and educational programs in this house is to raise awareness of the many ways of being Jewish in history and the present day – be it Orthodox, Reform Judaism, Zionism or secular Judaism and Jewish culture. And, of course, we want to emphasize that Jewish history in Germany is not a closed chapter but an ongoing story. Immigration from Ukraine, Russia and the Baltic states has produced living communities but also many new questions on Jewish future in our country.

We have never had enough resources for research. But one special exhibition we presented in spring 2010 was an important step we are proud of: we were able to tell the stories of 24 Jewish immigrants of the last 20 years who all came from the former Soviet Union. These people – religious, atheist, liberal, orthodox, conservative, Lubavitcher, children and elderly people, WW II veterans and young IT professionals – are broadening the spectrum of Jewish identities in Germany again. As they form the majority of the present-day Jewish communities we are obliged to take note of their experiences and perspectives. Their way of life is completely different from those we knew before, and we try to embed these eastern European stories into the picture of Judaism we communicate here.

Volunteering and professionalism
The Jewish Museum of Westphalia is not a public institution. This is why most members of the staff are volunteers. The museum is run by an association of about 500 individuals and corporations who bear a large part of the budget. But, of course, we can count on support by the town administration, the regional and state authorities and some foundations, sometimes also by companies from this town. And the private character of this museum is, as visitors express, something one can feel in what we are doing. Nevertheless, many experts have judged that our activities – special exhibitions on arts and history, educational programs, research and publications – can be seen as "state of the art". We are convinced that both – volunteering and professional standards – can meet and that this status will enable us for future development and intelligent answers to new questions.

Johanna Eichmann / Elisabeth Cosanne-Schulte-Huxel

From Dorsten to Chicago
The History of the Eisendrath Family in Dorsten

"The family name is one of which every Eisendrath can be well proud. Its record has been good; all of its members have been known as honest citizens; and its name has never been dragged into courts or been identified with anything that would degrade the name 'Eisendrath'." This is a quotation from a thesis written by Ruth Eisendrath in Chicago in 1931.

We'll have to contradict here a little, as Samson Nathan Eisendrath appears in a police-case report in 1837 and had to pay a penalty of 15 silver-pennies. "Because he had pumped water from the dye-works during the holidays". There were also arguments within the Jewish community in Dorsten, which made court warrants necessary.
And here we are, already in the middle of the history of the Eisendrath family. First of all let's go back to the beginnings of the Jewish community in Dorsten.

A newspaper article in 1932 reports the existence of Jews in Dorsten as early as the 13th century. "They were wealthy, respected and very religious", was noted. "In spite of their popularity among fellow citizens, the bishop in Münster ordered his officials to expel all Jews from the diocese. (…). In the following years entry permits were rarely granted."
Up to now we have not been able to confirm that Jewish people had already lived in Dorsten in the 13th century. It seems strange indeed that another detail of this article from 1932 says that the Jews in Dorsten built a "fine synagogue" and established their own cemetery around 1750. If this is correct, it seems peculiar that only 60 years later these facts were unknown.

As a matter of fact in 1816 the chairman of the district council, the Earl of Westerholt, ordered Dorsten's mayor Gahlen, "within 14 days, to report everything about the synagogues and schools of the Israelites in your mayoral boundaries, also of their qualifications, salary and the number of pupils etc. "Extensive report necessary", the mayor noted at the bottom of the letter.

"6 families. No synagogue, prayer service is held in one of Nathan (Eisendrath's) rooms. No school, instead a room. Abraham Isaak is the teacher. 8 pupils."

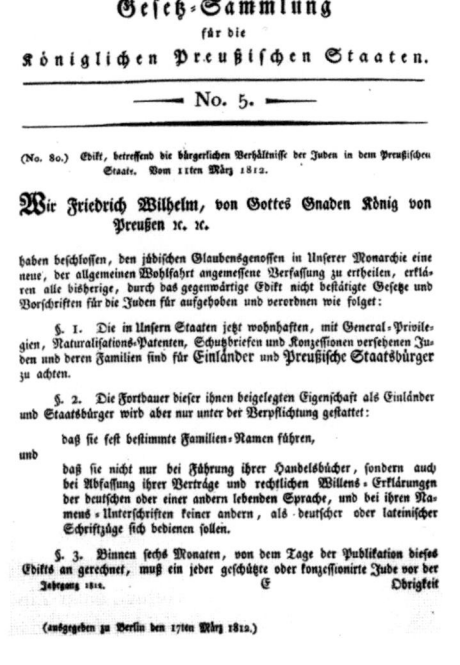

After more than a thousand years of being outlawed and confined to ghettos, the Jews sensed their hour of freedom with the coming of the age of enlightment. For Prussian Jews – Dorsten belonged to Prusssia since 1813 – the change came with the edict of March 11th 1812 "Concerning the civic circumstances of the Jews". Among others it is noted here: "Those Jews and their families now living in our state are to be respected as Prussian citizens. Extremely important is also the introduction of the liberty to exercise a trade. Traders were immediately freed from the necessity of belonging to a (Christian!) guild. They just had to purchase a traders permit, to which every citizen of integrity, had a right". The edict gave the Jewish community rights, the right to vote, the liberty to exercise a trade, the right to settle wherever they please and also allowed them to take up an academic profession.

The edict of emancipation was received enthusiastically in the progressive groups of Jewish society. The Jewish magazine "Sulamith", for example, said: "On March 11th (1812) began a new favourable era for our fellow believers in the state of Prussia. The achievement of citizens rights, the equalization of our fellow believers with the rest of the states' population, has brought a new spirit among the Israelites, and our whole influence and endeavour has received a totally different perspective". These exuberant expectations were soon shown to be an illusion, as the emancipation laws were not accepted by everyone. In 1822, the King prohibited Jews to become teachers in Prussia and dismissed them from all government service. This Prussian prohibition remained until 1850, so that the Jews, as before, were only left with professions looked down upon like second hand dealing, peddling, pawnbroking, and cattle and corn trading. Furthermore, they were allowed to go in for small scale industry: many Jews then became jewellers, sales clerks at trade fairs, leather and textile merchants.

The first important question arose on the subject of citizens rights. Who was entitled to Prussian citizenship? Due to the confusion caused by the Napoleonic wars, Dorsten had changed its nationality several times, until in 1815, it was finally attributed to Prussia at the Congress of Vienna.
If there was Jewish immigration, it was necessary to define their qualifications for Prussian citizenship. A decree from March 19th 1819 improved the situation after 1815, but didn't permit a further immigration of "foreign/stranger" Jews.

The royal government of the interior in Münster decreed on November 23rd 1823 that the local authorities must," strictly observe that under no maxim, are "foreign" Jews again to "sneak in". Due to the fact that not enough attention was paid to this rule, the royal government of the interior issued the following instructions to its subordinate authorities on October 30th 1827: "Under threat of a severe penalty for the mayor, it is not allowed without our permission, to admit foreign Jews as businessmen, commercial travellers, domestic servants or similar to stay in our country. This is necessary to avoid them 'squatting', which itself brings huge problems".

The official language here shows us the extent of the phobia that considered the Jews as unwanted "aliens" and "intruders".

In 1808, the first Jews in Dorsten received their permission to settle. These were the 45-year-old butcher David Moyses from Wesel, who later took the name of Perlstein, and 43 years old Michel Samuel from Mülheim/Ruhr, also a butcher, who later took the name Grünebaum. In the Dorsten council`s letter requesting permission to settle for Michel Samuel, it is clear, which conditions are necessary or even hoped for. "Evidence of his good conduct and his good manners" on the one side, but particularly - the opinion of the mayor – that "competition among the butchers should be beneficial for the city of Dorsten".

Five further families followed until 1812, among those was Samson Nathan Eisendrath from Haltern. His profession was "merchant"; he was the only Prussian Jew. Within four to five years a small Jewish community with eight families was founded in Dorsten. This small community didn't just have the usual problems of survival attributed to a business foundation, but also those experienced in an atmosphere where Jews were not just seen as "strangers" but as religious outsiders in a strict Catholic township.

The everyday language of Jews in Dorsten was Yiddish, the so called Jewish German, as seen in the incomprehensible German in letters of complaint from these times. Two parties soon formed in Dorsten. The "progressives" with Samson Nathan Eisendrath as chairman of the community on the one hand and the orthodox or the "zealots" on the other, which included the founding fathers of the community: David Moyses (Perlstein) and Michel Samuel (Grünebaum).

On June 15th 1820, mayor Gahlen received a letter of complaint with the following content: since 1808 men have been meeting for worship in an orderly furnished prayer room which they call a "synagogue". The warden is the merchant David Moyses who belongs to the "zealots" group. Since Easter 1820 "a disturbance took place" though, because Samson Nathan's group has been having their own "church-going". From

1817 Samson Nathan was synagogue warden. He organized the prayer service, arranged the use of a room in his home and provided a Thora scroll. But these were difficult times. Tradition was not taken for granted. The slowly progressing emancipation of the Jews led to changes, which questioned the past and present concept of the community. The quarrels between both groups increased.

Being a mediator in this case was too much for the mayor of Dorsten and therefore he requested the help of the responsible regional rabbi, Abraham Sutro of Münster. As in the meantime "there has even been violence in the synagogue itself", Sutro travelled to Dorsten. His attempts at mediation failed, with the result that the differences in the community increased. When mayor Gahlen wanted to collect the contribution towards the travel expenses from Samson Eisendrath, he refused because the regional rabbi had not sufficiently settled the points of issue". The stressed mayor, who had been asked to help, requested advice from his superior authority. "How can I prosecute these stubborn people?"

The Dorsten community didn't calm down in the following two decades and eventually things came to a climax. On April 14th 1844, Samson Nathan Eisendrath laid down his warden's position, which he had held for 27 years. Unfortunately, no precise reasons for this can be found, but probably the conflict between the "law abiding" Jews and the "modernizers" had escalated.

Three years later, on April 23rd 1847, Eisendrath gave notice of his withdrawal from the synagogue community, with his four sons David (1816 /28 years), Moses (1820/24 years), Cosmann (1825/19 years) and Osea or Oscar/Asser 1827/17 years). He let the community have both of his Torah scrolls and drapes, emphasizing, though, that the "synagogue utensils" are his "own property". He and his sons still wanted to attend the synagogue, but "voluntarily" when they wanted to without being counted on to form a minion.

It was only after the Prussian law of July 23rd 1847, which stated that every Jew had to belong to the community and pay taxes, that the Jewish community was able to develop a working administration under the supervision of the state. It remained orthodox. It is not known, however, whether the many years of conflict were connected with the general religious differences among German Jewry. The name Eisendrath appeared in the new statutes in 1857.

These are the beginnings of the Jewish Community in Dorsten, and they play a decisive role in the story of Samson Nathan Eisendrath and his family.

Samson Nathan was born in Haltern on February 18th 1785. He was the only Jew who came from the Prussian area. He seems to have come via Amsterdam though. In 1810/1811 he received permission to settle in Dorsten. After the birth of their first child Baruch, in Amsterdam 1812, his wife Julia followed him to Dorsten. Other family members followed. First of all, Julia's mother Edel Abraham, Abraham Isaak came next. He was a teacher and probably a relation of Julia's. His main subject as a teacher was religion. Mayor Luck called him "a worn out old man" and said that Samson Nathan saw in him "less of a teacher, more a chance of receiving his 1000 Reichstalers fortune which he was due to inherit as there were no children".

The first records only mention Samson Nathan. The name Eisendrath appeared later. According to a cabinet resolution of the Prussian government from 1845 all Jews had to have an hereditary name. Samson Nathan declared that he and his family would have the name Eisendrath which he had already been using for many years. The name Eisendrath is very unusual and the family interprets it as follows "Eisen (iron)" as

26

the hardest metal and "drath (wire)" as the limb that holds the family together. The name is supposed to symbolize great power and unity.

Samson Nathan's registered profession of "Handelsmann" (merchant) doesn't say much about what he really did. In the trade tax records of 1828 several professions were noted: apart from butcher and shopkeeper of haberdashery, tanner and candlemaker were mentioned.

Business probably prospered as Samson Nathan's family soon settled down in Dorsten. At first, they lived outside the city wall but Samson Nathan soon bought a large piece of land on Wiesen Strasse close to the market place and later purchased other lots as well. In a survey from 1830, four lots were registered under Nathan Eisendrath's name. For seventy years the house at 357 Wiesen Strasse, located close to the synagogue, was the centre of the Eisendrath family's life and business. A census from 1828 recorded 16 people living in Samson Nathan Eisendrath's house.

American records described Samson Nathan as a "jovial person, homeloving and congenial. He loved card-playing and drinking because they encouraged a friendly and informal atmosphere. Therefore it was not unusual for him to invite travelling merchants to his house and have them stay with him for several days; during these visits Samson and his guests would play solo continually for two or three days and nights."

And here another detail about him. He was decorated three times by the King of Prussia, decorated upon the birth of each seventh child. Then there is an incident often related as to how one day he returned from a trip and when one of his youngest sons, very small at that time, ran up to him to embrace him, throwing his chubby arms around his father's skins, Samson flattered by such affection, leaned down and patted the youngster on the head inquiring, "Now, little one, pray whose child are you?"

There is a little doubt regarding the number of sons and daughters. Our research shows just 18 births, in the archives though American scholars mention 23 children. Fact is: when an official will was made in 1855,

Julia and Samson Nathan Eisendrath spoke of 11 children still alive. In this mutual will they say:

"From our marriage have come forth 11 children, of which seven namely

1.   Baruch resident in Amsterdam,
2.   David resident here in Dorsten,
3.   Moses resident here in Dorsten,
4.   Levi resident in Laer,
5.   Nathan resident in America,
6.   Oskar resident here in Dorsten,
7.   Jeanette, wife of Moses Rosenthal resident in Waltrop,
have received at their marriage, goods or money to the value of more than 200 Prussian talers.

The other four of our children namely:
8.   Cosmann resident here in Dorsten,
9.   Benjamin resident here in Dorsten,
10.   Adelheid resident here in Dorsten,
11.   Eva resident here in Dorsten,
are to receive the sum of 200 Prussian talers when we die".

After the introduction of schools in Prussia the authorities saw that Jewish children were also correctly educated. If the Jewish community was unable to provide its own school, the children had a right to visit the Christian schools. They just had to provide for religious lessons. In 1820 rabbi Sutro had already demanded for a Jewish community teacher to be employed for the children of the eight Jewish families in Dorsten. However, they refused to pay for the teachers' salary and food because most of them were poor. After a dispute lasting three years, the following was agreed on: with the help of two house and family fathers, who were to be elected, Samson Nathan Eisendrath was appointed to engage a teacher, collect school fees and decide on the order in which families would take it in turns to provide accommodation and food for the teacher.

295	Eisendrath, Abraham	Amsterdam	1857	VI	Diamanten-makler	Amsterdam
	Eisendrath, Baruch	Dorsten	1863	VI	Leder-fabrikant	Racine, Wisconsin
	Eisendrath, Hermann	Amsterdam	1863	VI	Sortimenter	Amsterdam
	Eisendrath, Levi	Dorsten	1829	VII	-	Laar (†)
	Eisendrath, Nathan	-	1835	VII	Rentner	Chicago († 18.IV.1902)

Samson Nathan Eisendrath was quite a progressive man for those times. He sent his children to the Petrinum Grammar school (Baruch, Levi and Nathan are recorded here), Eva visited the Ursulinen Grammar school, Oskar became a butcher, Cosmann a trader, Levi, Moses and David merchants. David also became a candlemaker and Moses a tanner.

He also ambitiously supported the education and training of other Jewish children. He was responsible for the Marks-Haindorf-Foundation – an association for the promotion of Jewish artisans. Dr. Alexander Haindorf (1784 – 1862) was the founder. "In the first 50 years the foundation was able to provide apprenticeships for 350 Jewish boys, also in Dorsten (…) There were eight apprentices learning their trade in 1833, in hosiery, as a cobbler and a turner". Haindorf wasn't very happy with these professions, though.

He advised Mayor Luck to "let the apprentices learn manual professions such as locksmith or bricklayer". Luck thought this to be too difficult, "as the local boys are weak and dwarf like". Samson Nathan also looked after the education of the sons of poorer Jews, organized apprenticeships and in an emergency, clothing, board and "bedclothes".

When Samson Nathan died in 1857 at 72, his wife Julia was 64 years old. She survived her husband by 21 years. The descendants say that she was the matriarch who was the boss in the family. She was proud and very self-confident, they say. But above all she worked very hard and must have been a remarkable housewife who managed to run such a complicated household in the Wiesen Strasse.

The Eisendrath family was welded together, the older brothers and sisters cared for the youngsters, and this worked the other way around. The oldest son Baruch lived in Amsterdam and died while visiting his mother in Dorsten 1874. Son Oskar died in 1855 from liver disease; the other nine children emigrated one after the other, with their families to the U.S.

The twenty five year old Nathan emigrated in 1848 on the ship "Preussen" via Rotterdam. After the annulment of the Prussian anti–emigration laws, hundreds of thousands were going this way. In the late 1840's, there was a long economic crisis, and there was mass emigration. Refugees from all over Europe flock to the main ports: one estimates about 44 million, among those 5.5 million Germans between 1821 and 1914.

After several different places Nathan Eisendrath finally settled in Chicago in 1853, he was a successful entrepreneur, he helped his nieces and nephews emigrate and gave them jobs in the family business. The German – American Biographical Publishing Company notes, 1901 – 1902: "Nathan Eisendrath belongs to the most senior businessmen in Chicago. After the pioneer period with all its difficulties, he never gave up, and while building his own fortune, he supported the growth and prosperity of the City..... In 1853 he established his soap factory. In this branch, he was so successful, that in 1856 he found partners and opened up a bank". He also had shares in several other enterprises such as liquor and groceries. Nathan and his brothers Cosmann and Moses were co-founders of the Sholom temple (North Chicago Hebrew Congregatio).

By 1880, eight further brothers and sisters had emigrated with their families to the U.S. Nathan Eisendrath was primarily the contact person. The family clan achieved high levels of standard in several branches. If you had mentioned the name of Eisendrath in the U.S. one hundred years ago, you would have been connected to the leather industry. The Eisendraths had gone a long way in this field, from the beginnings as a tanner in Dorsten to one of the top representatives in the U.S.

Benjamin was considered too weak for military service in 1857, so he worked for many years in the meat packing business, Moses in the grocery trade and David in the leather industry. We also find well known architects, wholesalers, photographers and many more among the professions of the Eisendraths'.

Mother Julia Eisendrath died on February 23rd 1878. The eulogy was spoken by the High Rabbi Dr. Horowitz from Krefeld.

What had kept these brothers and sisters, who emigrated to the States, together? Ruth Eisendrath said in 1931: "… The six brothers and three sisters were all short in height, had typically stocky German builds and were all of ruddy complexion. Mentally they were all known to be alert, active and intelligent, while temperamentally they have even been described as easy-going, jovial and phlegmatic."

"The Eisendrath's conception and philosophy of life is almost entirely idealistic. The men, for the most part, aside from being serious-minded, hard-working and ambitious persons are rather overly trusting; they are always willing to help a friend out, and always sympathize most sincerely after hearing a hard luck story, never doubting its veracity. This feeling is rather the outgrowth of the old traditional spirit of "all for one and one for all".

They have always kept up the contacts to Dorsten and their relations in the Netherlands. Two plaques at the rear of the entrance remind us that the Wolff and Eisendrath families renovated the Jewish cemetery in Dorsten in 1910 and 1922. Joseph Eisendrath noted that American visitors in 1928 invited the Eisendrath and Wolff families to a grand lobster dinner in Cologne.

The family kept their eye on German politics from America. In a protest letter to President Hindenburg in 1933, the "Eisendrath Cousins Club" complained about the treatment of "Germans of the Jewish faith". Here a quote: "Because of my German ancestry, which goes back many centuries, my concern and sense of justice, I appeal to you today to help the German Jews who are being treated so miserably by some political aspirants of your beloved country....".

What happened to the Jewish community in Dorsten in these times? By 1899 the figure was strongly diminished. Prayer service was, as a rule, impossible due to the lack of men. The upcoming neighbourhoods of the Ruhr district such as Gelsenkirchen, Gladbeck and Bottrop had been considered much more attractive than rural Dorsten. In 1925 only 25 members of the Jewish community were left. In 1932 there were 47 members. On January 23rd 1942, the last 12 Jewish citizens were deported to the ghetto in Riga. That was the end of the Jewish community in Dorsten - to the present day.

46 descendants of Baruch Eisendrath's family in the Netherlands lost their lives in the concentration camps.

"The effect of an urban environment upon a large family group", is how Ruth Eisendrath titled her thesis about 80 years after the first emigration surge to the U.S. Today, 80 years on, a further sociological study of the family Eisendrath would be interesting.

Sources
Ruth Eisendrath: The effect of an urban environment upon a large family group, Chicago 1931
Archive of the Jewish Museum of Westphalia, Dorsten
City Archive, Dorsten
Archive of Petrinum High School, Dorsten
Private Archives Family Eisendrath

Josef Ulfkotte

Jewish life in a small Westphalian town two hundred years ago

When the name Eisendrath first appeared in Dorsten in 1811, the people of the town could already look back on 560 years of town history. It was Konrad von Hochstaden who as Archbishop of Cologne and ruler granted the village of Dorsten city rights on 1 June 1251. Thus the people of the town received the right to build a wall and a moat around Dorsten to help protect the town from attacks. The medieval layout of the town with the market place, the weigh house, the parish church and the fortifications are still visible in the present-day townscape. By giving Dorsten town status, the Archbishop of Cologne was also pursuing the aim of securing the north-west edge of the area he ruled against attacks from the neighbouring territories. The area he ruled directly bordered the prince-bishopric of Münster and the Duchy of Cleves. The Archbishop of Cologne ruled Dorsten up to 1803.

The farming communities of Durstina and Durstinon formed the nucleus of the town of Dorsten. The settlement of Durstina developed around 100 CE *(Common Era)* on the north bank of the Lippe, the isolated farm settlement of Durstinon around 500 CE *(Common Era)* on the south bank of the river.

For 60 years the area around the Lippe near Dorsten-Holsterhausen has been an important archaeological site with finds that provide insight into the history of the Roman Empire under Emperor Augustus. Between 1999 and 2006 before the development of a large, new residential area, archaeologists were able to carry out a detailed study on a total of 160,000 square metres of land. The main result of these excavations, which started again a few weeks ago, was the discovery of more Roman marching camps which the Romans built on the Lippe in order to also gain control of Germania which, up to then, had been free. After their defeat in 9 CE, the base at Dorsten-Holsterhausen became insignificant for the Romans.

Around the year 50 CE Germanic settlements developed on the soil of the old sites and finds dating back to the 5th century have been made.

The favourable, geographical location on a river and on the crossroads of several trading routes was a major factor in the economic rise of the town in the centuries after being granted city status. In the 15th century five markets as well as a weekly market were held regularly. For some time the town also had a mint. Wood, livestock as well as textiles and leather goods characterised local trade. The weekly Dorsten corn market was the only weekly corn market in the northwestern area ruled by the Archbishop of Cologne, the Vest Recklinghausen. The border town character of the town and its location on a major Lippe crossing were the main reasons why Dorsten was so often drawn into the disputes of the neighbouring countries and rulers. And the town's possessions on the northern bank of the Lippe meant a permanent feud with the noble neighbours in the Münsterland. The Lippe was both a bridge and a border.

At the time of the Reformation initiated by Martin Luther in 1517, the people of Dorsten remained loyal to the Pope and the Catholic Church. Also in 1582, when the Archbishop of Cologne became Protestant and tried to convert the people by force, they did not change their position. The situation became difficult for the town in the Thirty Years War which was fought in wide areas of central Europe from 1618 up to the Peace Treaties of Münster and Osnabrück, the so-called "Peace of Westphalia" in 1648. In 1633 the Protestant Landgrave of Hesse-Cassel occupied the Catholic town of Dorsten and developed it into a strong fortress. Eight years later the Catholics recaptured the town which did not recover from the effects of the Thirty Years War until modern times. The Seven Years War, which lasted from 1756 to 1763, also did a lot of damage. In the storming of the town, which was occupied by the French, 30 houses and barns went up in flames. The damage was quite considerable but relatively mild compared to the damage caused by the bombing of the town on 22 March 1945, thus shortly before the end of the Second World War, when within a very short space of time 80 percent of the old part of town was destroyed.

In 1488 the Franciscan Order established a cloister in Dorsten which still exists today. In 1641 the Hessians were driven out and in 1642, together with the town of Dorsten, the Franciscans established the Gymnasium Petrinum *(a high school)*. The school now looks back on a 370-year history. This school was also attended by some children of the Eisendrath family.

While the Franciscans saw to the education of the boys, the Ursulines who came to Dorsten in 1699, educated the girls. There has been close co-operation between the Gymnasium Petrinum and the St. Ursula Gymnasium for many years now. Coeducation has existed for about forty years. Apart from the Gymnasium, the Ursuline Order also runs another secondary school exclusively for girls. At the beginning of the 20th century the Franciscans founded a college for training young monks. The college existed until the start of the Second World War.

In 1887 a third order settled in Dorsten that was dedicated to the care of the sick. This Catholic order, the Brothers of Mercy of Montabaur, established a clinic and hospital outside the city gates for physically and mentally handicapped people. In 1937 the National Socialists, whose ideology denied the handicapped the right to exist, drove the order from the town. The patients did not survive.

After Napoleon's downfall and the redrawing of Europe at the Congress of Vienna in 1814/15, a new era started for Dorsten. Dorsten was then ruled by the King of Prussia who governed his land from Berlin. The first Protestants came to our town in 1816 when the Royal Prussian District Court was established. In the 19th century the number of Protestants steadily grew so that at the end of the 19th century the Protestant Christians were able to build their own church. Apart from the Catholics and Protestants, a Jewish community was also established in the 19th century.

Up to the middle of the 19th century, shipbuilding was very important for Dorsten. For many years the "Dorstener Aak", a small, flexible barge, which was especially suitable for shipping on the Lippe, sold very well in the Netherlands. In order to improve its navigability, in the 18th century the Lippe was regulated and 12 locks were built. The development of roads after 1850 and the construction of railways from 1874 to 1880 meant that the Lippe was no longer the only means of transportation and the competition was just too much. In 1876 all transport of commercial goods on the Lippe stopped. From 1880 three railway lines connected the Lippe area around Dorsten with the "big, wide world" and encouraged entrepreneurs to establish large industrial enterprises. In 1930 a canal running parallel to the Lippe was opened. It was and still is an important transport route for bulk goods.

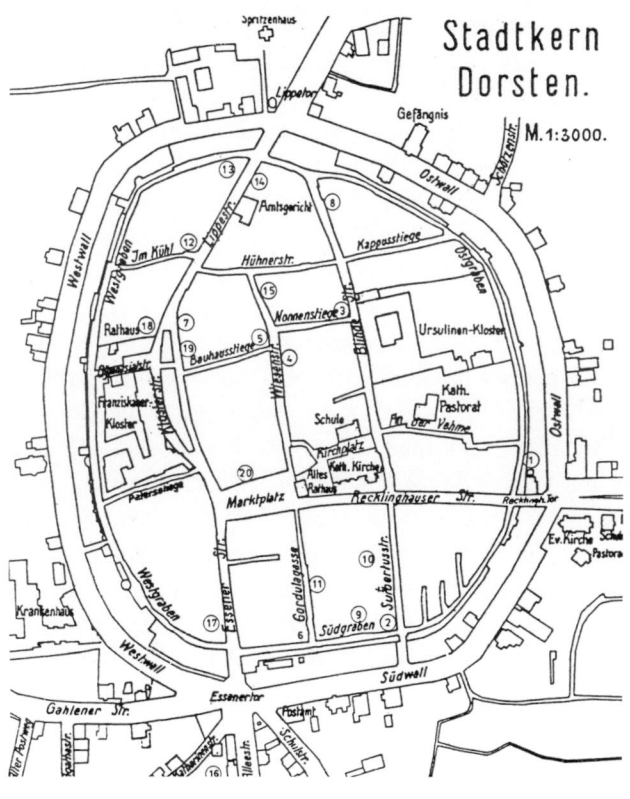

Since the Middle Ages the villages of Holsterhausen and Hervest had developed in the north of the town behind the opposite bank of the Lippe and they kept their village character right up to the end of the 19th century. But after the turn of the century they turned into mining communities within just twenty years with more than two thirds of the inhabitants dependent on the mines. The establishment of the first industrial enterprises and the start of coal production led to a rise in the population

37

in Holsterhausen and Hervest from 1651 inhabitants in 1900 to 14421 inhabitants in 1930 while the increase in population in the old part of Dorsten was much lower, namely from 3336 in 1885 to 8897 in 1928. The two mines north of the Lippe, which started coal production in 1914 shortly before the start of the First World War, increased their workforce in the next decade from 1600 to 4800 miners. A high percentage of the miners, who now lived in the mining estates established especially for them not far from the villages of Holsterhausen and Hervest, were of East German descent. Their language, customs and habits were different to those of the indigenous population and this led to tension between the people living on the estates and the villagers whose families had always lived there. Today, that is about 100 years later, the two mines in the north of Dorsten no longer exist. The "Baldur" mine in Holsterhausen was already closed in 1931 and Fürst Leopold, which was located in Hervest, stopped production in 2001. In the "European Capital of Culture" year of 2010, only six working mines remained in the Ruhr, the region which once had the most mines in the whole of Europe. The redevelopment of the sites of old mines is a major challenge for the town of Dorsten.

The Eisendraths had left the town long before 1914 when the First World War started. Our history books say that this war was the "seminal catastrophe of the 20th century". Towards the end of the war the German Reich was shaken by major political upheavals which also affected Dorsten. This also applied to Hervest and Holsterhausen which were working class areas. Fights between supporters of the revolutionary Spartacus League resp. the Communist Party and the Freikorps, i.e. volunteer corps, which the government made use of to crush the uprisings in the Ruhr, characterised the first post-war years north and south of the Lippe. In January 1923 French and Belgian soldiers occupied the Ruhr area as a reprisal because in the opinion of France, which was the victorious power, Germany had failed to fulfil reparation payments to be made to France as demanded by the Versailles Treaty. For the next two years Dorsten was occupied by the Belgians who ensured the transportation of coal and other industrial products from the Ruhr to France. Inflation, which reached its peak all over the country in autumn 1923, ruined the existence of many businesses and destroyed the assets of the many small savers in Dorsten too. Some seven years later the middle and lower income groups were again hit hard. As a result of the Great Depression many people in Dorsten also lost their jobs after 1930. In Hervest and especially Holsterhausen, where between 1900 and 1930 the new mines had led to a huge rise in the population, the economic misery was particularly high. In 1933 a total of 3,705 job-seekers were registered in Hervest and Holsterhausen. The Communist propaganda also influenced the people of Hervest and Holsterhausen which in the 1920s increasingly developed into strongholds of the Communist Party. Until it dissolved in July 1933, the Centre Party, the party of the Catholic population, was by far the strongest party in the old part of town. The German elections in March 1933 were the last free elections to be held in Germany before the Second World War. While on a national level the Nazis received 44% of the votes cast, in Dorsten the percentage of votes they received was considerably lower: Dorsten (old town) 30.1%, Hervest: 26.8%, Holsterhausen: 16.6%. The results show that there was definitely no great enthusiasm for the Nazi party and Hitler. Nationally, however, the Nazis came to power even if it was only in a coalition with the German National People's Party, the DNVP. Did the voters in Dorsten have any idea what Hitler's rule would lead to? That is highly unlikely. Hitler was underestimated in Dorsten and other places. At first things improved in Dorsten, as in the whole of Germany. But this was pure deceit. After Hitler was sure that nobody could oppose his power, he mobilized all the forces to prepare the way for world domination by what he called the "Aryan race".

In his programmatic book "Mein Kampf" he had already named the Jews as his worst enemies and said that if he came to power he would "deal with them without mercy". This also applied to the Jews of Dorsten and neighbouring communities.

As early as 31 May 1933, thus just about two weeks after the last free elections in the German Reich, SA men and young people in uniform distributed leaflets in the streets in which a boycott of shops owned by Jews was ordered for Saturday 1 April. From 10 a.m. the next day SA and SS men in uniform were posted outside Jewish stores. In their hands they held signs saying: "Germans, don't buy in Jewish stores." People were at a loss when they saw the attacks by the SA and some were disgusted. In the old part of town Amalie Perlstein decorated the inside of her store window with a picture of her son Otto who died serving his country as a soldier in the First World War. At the same time SA men were sticking signs to the outside of the store window which said that the store belonged to a Jew. In Hervest an SA troop stormed the ladies' and men's wear store that belonged to Joseph Silver, a Jew who had moved from Bielefeld to Dorsten in 1927. Faced with the choice of either being shot dead or closing his store, he emigrated to Palestine in 1933. Other Jews thought that Mr. Silver was a pessimist and believed that things would soon change for the better. Many later paid for their earlier optimism with their lives. More and more laws and orders were passed that discriminated against Jews. In November 1938, 30 men in uniform devastated the synagogue on Wiesen Strasse and then burned all the furniture and sacral objects on the market place. Just a few weeks after the pogrom the Jews had to vacate their homes and move to buildings designated and marked as Jewish houses, in German "Judenhäuser". The Jewish community house on Wiesen Strasse and Hildegard Perlstein's house on Lippe Strasse became

Judenhäuser. Soon any contact with "Aryan" families was banned. Occasionally Dorsten businesspeople secretly gave them food or items of clothing. When in 1942 the last Jews were driven out of their houses for deportation to the places where they were then murdered, the neighbours stood at their doors and cried. After 21 January 1942 no more Jews lived in Dorsten.

During the Second World War a large number of camps were set up in Dorsten for prisoners of war from France, Poland and the Soviet Union who were forced to work in firms in

Dorsten. The Nazis also abducted young women from Poland and the Soviet Union to Germany where as forced labourers they were made to work in ammunition factories or on farms, also in Dorsten. The farmers in particular appreciated the help of the forced labourers. They had problems running their farms as most men were in the army or had been killed. Thus they often treated the forced labourers like members of their families. There were, of course, also cases of oppression and harassment so that after Germany had been liberated from the National Socialist dictatorship, the forced labourers unleashed their fury on their tormentors. Shortly before the end of the war, Dorsten was finally reduced to ashes by the bombs dropped by the Allies.

The war ended on 8 May 1945 and it took many years for the people of Dorsten to remove the scars of the war and build up the town again. It did not take long for new challenges to come. The ethnic Germans expelled in 1945 from the areas east of the Oder–Neisse line, which now belonged to Poland, or from Czechoslovakia, had to be housed and integrated in the occupation zones of the Western Allies in Germany. In view of the food and housing shortages, this was a huge task which Dorsten also had to face. The people had no time to deal intensively with the events of the 12-year Nazi dictatorship because they were too busy trying to cope with the everyday difficulties. People preferred not to think of the "brown years" also in Dorsten until the early 80s when an action group formed whose aim was to study Dorsten under the Nazis. The result of the "Research Group Dorsten under the Swastika" is an impressive five-volume documentation which now forms the basis of all local history work on the Nazi period in Dorsten.

The special initiative of the "research group" also owes its development to the Jewish Museum of Westphalia in Dorsten. There are now 34 information points in Dorsten. One of them reminds us of the history of the Jews in our town, another of the forced labourers during the Second World War. We owe the so-called "Stumbling Stones" to the "Women for Peace" action group. The Stumbling Stones have been laid in recent years in front of some houses in the town in which Jews lived before they were deported.

Today Dorsten is a town in motion. The shortage of manpower about forty years ago gave many people from Turkey the opportunity to find work, also in Dorsten. Many of them live in our town with their children and grandchildren, particularly in Hervest where there are now two mosques. In recent years the immigration of Jews from Russia has lent Jewish life in our region new impetus. And in the last few decades some free churches have also established their places of worship.

The number of inhabitants is falling steadily. At present some 70,000 people live in our town which also has an aging population. The fall in the birth rate means that the authorities will have to consider whether to close down some schools. The huge debts that Dorsten has, mean that the town will have to restrict spending and make major cuts. This makes public involvement all the more necessary or to quote John F. Kennedy: "Those who act while others are still talking are a great step ahead in life."

Sources

Evelt, Jul(ius): Beiträge zur Geschichte der Stadt Dorsten und ihrer Nachbarschaft. In: Westfälische Zeitschrift. Zeitschrift für vaterländische Geschichte und Alterthumskunde 23 (1863), S. 1 - 95, 24(1864), S. 87 - 197, 26(1866), S. 63 - 176.

Forschungsgruppe Regionalgeschichte/Dorsten unterm Hakenkreuz (Hrsg.): Juden in Dorsten und in der Herrlichkeit Lembeck, Dorsten 1989.

Kuhlmann, Bernhard: Geschichte der Stadt Dorsten von der Zeitenwende bis zum Jahr 1975. Ein Sachbuch über die Entwicklung der Stadt, ihrer Bevölkerung und Wirtschaft, o J. u. O.

Barbara Seppi

A Walk through History with Julia Eisendrath

Dorsten, August 2010: For two hours I had the pleasure to be Julia Eisendrath, born Isaack. Ready and prettily dressed with a long black robe with white collar and a lovely white bonnet to cover my hair I could greet her great-grand children in Dorsten and have a walk through the city center, trying to male old times come alive.

We started in Wiesenstrasse, the road where Julia lived her lifetime since she came to Dorsten in 1811 together with her husband Samson Nathan Eisendrath. We stood in front of house Nr. 19, where Julia gave birth to 23 children and where she died after a fulfilled life 1878. The Eisendraths came to Dorsten after the Napoleon Laws from 1808 permitted Jewish Families to settle wherever they wanted. The restriction of former government of the Archbishop of Cologne had been dropped. Soon many families like the Eisendraths came to the little flourishing village of Dorsten and started their business as butchers, merchants of cattle, skin tanners and much more. The Jewish community soon became the hugest in the area, the Synagogue established also in Wiesenstrasse became center of the religious life. Nevertheless, the Jewish families sent their children to the Catholic schools of Dorsten. As early as 1699 Dorsten had a Girls School run by the convent of Ursuline nuns in Ursulastrasse, which is still there nowadays. Also the famous Grammar School for Boys run by the Franciscan Order since 1642 took many Jewish boys.

Continuing the visit through the center of Dorsten we stopped at the "Lippetor", the River Lippe Gate. For centuries the river had been cornerstone for wealth and prosperity of the city. Dorsten was part of the glorious Hanseatic League in the middle-ages, the alliance of merchants in Northern Europe reaching from Baltic States to England. Right at the Lippetor we could see also the first house bought by a Jewish family in 1808, the family Perlstein. The entire Jewish community of the 19th century in Dorsten was spread widely over the area of the centre, there was no Ghetto, the families were integrated in the social life. Memorable are the donations of Julia Eisendrath to finance the building of a Christian church and also the fact, that on her death-bed she was assisted by Catholic nuns. So we had a good look into the peaceful coexistence of the people of Dorsten during the lifetime of Julia Eisendrath.

To find their luck in the United States of America the last Eisendrath left Dorsten in 1888, so that at least in Dorsten, the family has no victims of the Holocaust to mourn about. But of course, this part of the history was not spared out in our walk through the city. In eight places in the centre cobblestones remind of the 30 people, who had been dismissed, deported and murdered in concentration camps. Dorsten today recalls the former citizens Walter Rosenbaum, Simon and Gertrud Anna Reifeisen, Family Perlstein, Hermann Levinstein, Family Ambrunn, Ernst and Louise Joseph, Family Schöndorf and Family Metzger by tagging the places, where they had lived, to the people who walk through the city.

Impressions

Elisabeth Cosanne-Schulte-Huxel/
Walter Schiffer

The Dorsten Jewish Cemetery

A document from the year 1628 mentions a "Jewish field". This is the oldest and, up to now, only reference to a medieval Jewish community in the town of Dorsten. The "Jewish field" is located in exactly the same place as the later Jewish cemetery.

It was as early as 1808 that Jews received the right to settle in the town and a small community formed very quickly. The oldest burial at this Jewish cemetery, of which there is any record, was in 1815. This was documented in a "Death Register of the Jews in Dorsten" which was started that year. From 1815 to 1875 some 75 people were buried. Among them were children and grandchildren of Julia and Samson Eisendrath.

In 1910 a fence was built around the cemetery "to protect the graves and lend a dignified appearance". The enclosure, put up that same year, consisted of a sturdy gate and brick pillars joined by an iron fence. Two plaques at the gate name the donors of the fence: the Eisendrath and Meyer Wolff families of Chicago. The entrance gate withstood the destruction after 1938. After 1945 the cemetery was restored, but many gravestones are missing. They had been stolen or destroyed. The cemetery had once been opened in the hope that this place would allow the Jewish community to have a permanent resting place for the deceased. The National Socialists destroyed this hope.

The stone witnesses are the last traces of Jewish life in the town but the tombs at the Jewish cemetery were in danger of falling into a state of disrepair. In 2003 on the occasion of 750th anniversary of the town rights, the Cologne University of Applied Sciences, Faculty of Conservation Sciences, made a study of the cemetery for the Jewish Museum of Westphalia. Thanks to donations raised by the Michigan Foundation (Charles Eisendrath), it has been possible to conserve the tombstones of the Eisendrath family.

SAMSON NATHAN EISENDRATH

was born in Haltern on 18 February 1785 and died in Dorsten on 17 May 1857. Samson Nathan does not seem to have moved here directly from Haltern but from Amsterdam. Shortly after the first Jews had received permission to live and work in Dorsten (1808) Samson Nathan was the third Jew to receive a residence permit. In 1812, after the birth of their first child Baruch in Amsterdam, his wife Julia followed him to Dorsten. The occupation "merchant" provides very little information on his professional activities. In the 1828 list of businesses several are stated: apart from butcher also shopkeeper with haberdashery and Nuremberg products as well as clothmaker and dyer.

The family first lived outside the town wall but it was not long until Samson Nathan bought a large piece of land in Wiesen Strasse close to the market place and later various other plots too. For some 70 years the house on Wiesen Strasse, not far from the synagogue, was the residential and business centre of the Eisendrath family. In a census conducted in 1828, 16 people were mentioned as living in Samson Nathan Eisendrath's household.

Samson Nathan Eisendrath developed into one of the most important members of the Jewish community in Dorsten which he led from 1817 onwards. He arranged the services and provided a room in his house where the services could be held. He also acquired a Torah scroll. He was a co-author of the first statutes of the Jewish community in Dorsten but it was also Samson Nathan Eisendrath who caused the split in the synagogue. He was a religious and pugnacious man in religious matters.

For those times Samson Nathan Eisendrath was a very progressive man. He sent his children to the Gymnasium Petrinum (high school); (there are records that Baruch, Levi and Nathan attended the school). Eva attended the Ursuline School, Oskar trained to be a butcher, Cosman became a trader, and Levi, Moses and David were merchants and David also a candle maker. But he also did a lot to support the education and training of other Jewish children. The Marks-Haindorf-Stiftung, an association for the promotion of Jewish artisans, was particularly important to him and for many years he was the treasurer.

In 1845 the cabinet of the Prussian government decided that all Jews must take a family name. Samson Nathan declared that he and his family would take the name Eisendrath, the name he had been using for many years. The name Eisendrath is an unusual name and in the family it is interpreted as follows: "Eisen" (iron) as the hardest metal and "drath" (wire) as the bond which holds the family together. The name is meant to symbolise great strength and unity.

Nachdem in Gemäßheit der über die Verpflichtung der Juden zur Führung festbestimmter und erblicher Familiennamen ergangenen Allerhöchsten Kabinets-Ordre vom 31 October 1845 der *—Samson—* *Abraham Eisendrath* vor der Polizei-Obrigkeit seines Wohnorts *Dorsten* im Kreise *Recklinghausen*, erklärt hat, den Namen *—Eisendrath—* ferner als Familiennamen führen zu wollen, so wird Solches von der unterzeichneten Königlichen Regierung genehmigt und darüber demselben für sich und seine Nachkommen dieser Ausweis ertheilt.

Münster, den / ten *Juli* 1846.

Königlich Preußische Regierung.

After the cabinet order of 31 October 1845 on the obligation of Jews to take a family name Samson Nathan Eisendraht declared before the police authorities of Dorsten, his place of residence, that he wishes to take the family name Eisendrath.
This has been approved by the Royal Government and this document permits him and his descendants to use this name.
Münster 1 July 1846
Royal Prussian Government
Picture: Prussian resolution from 1845 on taking the family name "Eisendrath"

In 1848 his son Nathan emigrated to America. He settled in Chicago, was commercially successful and gradually his eight siblings and their families followed him. In 1880 after the death of their mother, Eva Wolf Eisendrath was the last of the Eisendrath family to leave Dorsten. The attachment to Dorsten remained. In 1910 and 1922 the Meyer Wolff and Eisendrath families had the Jewish cemetery in Dorsten renovated. The plaques at the entrance to the Jewish Cemetery verify this.

Samson Nathan Eisendraht died on 17 May 1857 at 3 in the afternoon as is documented by the Registry Office of the Royal District Court of Dorsten.

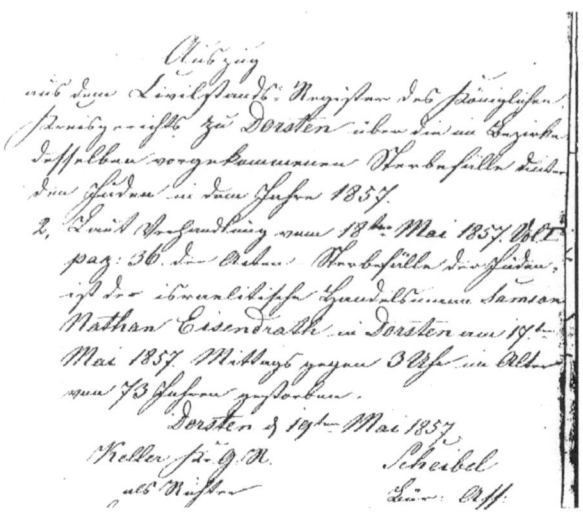

Extract from the Registry Office of the Royal District Court of Dorsten on the deaths of Jews in the year 1857 in this district.
2. Pursuant to the proceedings of 18th May 1857, vol. 1, p: 36 of the…..deaths of Jews, the Jewish merchant Samson Nathan Eisendrath died in Dorsten on 17 May 1857 at 3 in the afternoon at the age of 73.
Dorsten, 19 May 1857
Keller K. G.   Scheibel
Extract from Registry Office of the Royal District Court of Dorsten, Dorsten city archives

His epitaph reads:
Here lies buried
A man, sincere and upright
He went in sincerity, committed to righteousness,
Pious all his days
A righteous man who lived his belief
Shimshon, son of Nathan
Died at a very old age
On day 23 in Ijjar
Of the year 617 "according to the shortened Hebrew year"
"May his soul be bound up in the bonds of eternal life"

JULIA ISAAK EISENDRATH

Julia Isaak (also July/Güdla) was born on 19 October 1793. Her place of birth is not known. At a very young age she married Samson Nathan Eisendrath. In 1812 Baruch, their first son, was born in Amsterdam. In the following years many more children were born; we assume that there were 18 births. At the notarisation of a will on 13 February 1855, Julia and Samson Nathan Eisendrath speak of eleven living children (Baruch, David, Moses, Levi, Nathan, Oscar, Jeanette, Cosman, Benjamin, Adelheid and Eva).

The descendands of Julia say that she was a tiny person, even smaller than average. But she was extremely beautiful, had wonderful, white skin and slim, delicate hands. Her clothing was exquisite, if not to say extravagant. She always wore a lace bonnet with long ribbons as was proper for a Jewish wife. Her black taffeta dresses were "spruced up" with strikingly white lace collars and cuffs. Julia was also regarded as very generous and charitable, particularly to all the poor and needy. When a child was born she gave presents and donated money. She also donated to the Catholic sisters and for the bell in the new church. She let travelling merchants stay at their house a while and many nieces, nephews and grandchildren lived at the Eisendraths'. This hospitality remained with the family in Chicago. It was always an open house: "…. any person from the old country who had known the family over in Europe, was immediately taken into the homes".

The Eisendrath family was very close; the older siblings helped bring up the younger ones and supported each other. The family motto was: "All for one and one for all". The eldest son Baruch lived in Amsterdam and died in Dorsten in 1874 on a visit to his mother. Oscar died in 1855 from a liver disease and all the other 9 children gradually emigrated to the U.S. with their families.

Julia Eisendrath died on 23 February 1878. Shortly after this, the last daughter, Eva Eisendrath-Wolff, emigrated with her family to the U.S.

Den geehrten Bewohnern Dorsten's und Umgegend resp. allen Freunden und Bekannten zu unserer heutigen Abfahrt nach America ein herzliches

Lebewohl!

Dorsten, den 28. Mai 1880.
Meyer Wolff nebst Familie.

Today on our departure to America, we bid farewell to the dear people of Dorsten and surrounding area resp. to all friends and acquaintances.
Dorsten, 28 May 1880
Meyer Wolff and family

Farewell advertisement of family Meyer-Wolff / Eva Eisendrath in a Dorsten newspaper May 1880

They did not cut their links with Dorsten. Two plaques on the back of the entrance remind us that in 1919, 1922 and 2001 the Wolff and Eisendrath families had the Jewish cemetery renovated. Many family members, whether young or old, visited the Jewish cemetery in Dorsten und the tombs of their ancestors.

*Julia and Charles
Eisendrath, 1998*

The epitaph reads:

Here is buried
A woman, sincere and upright
She went on a perfect path
"It is" [1] Güdla, daughter of Yitzhak, wife of
Shimshon Eisendrath [2]
She passed away on the day of the "Holy Shabbat" on the "fourth" of the "fist" Adar [3]
Of the year 638 "according to the shortened Hebrew year"
"May her soul be bound up in the bonds of eternal life".

The eulogy was spoken by the High Rabbi Dr. Horowitz from Krefeld. Here one excerpt: "We have gathered here today in great grief and sorrow, at the bier bearing the coffin of a woman who, as is written in the quotations of our pious ancestors and patriarchs, 'grew old and was full of days', and who achieved something in her life which, in comparison

---

1 The abbreviation used here is ambiguous: it is the gracious or pious or dear etc. wife
2 Here there is a spelling mistake; here it says: Eisendraht
3 i.e. on the fourth day of Adar I

to her, few are privileged to achieve, and which goes far beyond the age which the psalmist grants man. May she depart this world in the knowledge that she has fulfilled beyond all measure the threefold holy duty of a woman, being wife and mother, person and Jewess. She had the great love of her family up to the very last day of her life. Her children carried this love with them over the coasts of the seas and over the borders of countries and treasured it in other parts of the world...".

BARUCH SAMSON EISENDRATH

was born on 8 July 1812 and was the oldest son of Julia Isaack and Samson Nathan. He and his siblings lived in Wiesen Strasse in the centre of Dorsten. In 1843, at the age of 31, he married Eva Abraham Witmondt (born 1823) in Amsterdam. She was the daughter of Abraham Hartog Witmondt and Marianne Hijmans Blitz. In the marriage documents it says that Eva Abraham is the owner of a library.

Baruch was a bookseller and his business address was: Oudenzijds Achterburgwal bij het Walenpleitje in Amsterdam. He imported German books and magazines, published novels and translated English, German and French books.

Eva and Baruch Eisendrath were married for 34 years and had 9 children: Marianna, Brunette, Abraham, Nathan, Sophia, Henri, Adelheid, Moritz and Samson.

> Heden beviel voorspoedig van een ZOON, EVIE WITMONDT, geliefde Echtgenoot van
> AMSTERDAM, 16 Augustus 1854.   B. EISENDRATH,
> (12479)   Boekhandelaar.

We happily announce the birth of a son born today to EVIE WITMONDT, beloved wife of B. Eisendrath, bookseller. Amsterdam, 16 August 1854

On the occasion of their 25ᵗʰ wedding anniversary on 10 August 1868,
their children placed the following announcement:
25-JARIGE ECHTVEREENIGING VAN
B. EISENDRATH
EN
E. WITMONDT.
HUNNE DANKBARE KINDEREN
Amsterdam, 10. Augustus 1868

25ᵗʰ WEDDING ANNIVERSARY OF
B. EISENDRATH
AND
E. WITMONDT.
THEIR GRATEFUL CHILDREN
Amsterdam, 10 August 1868

Baruch Eisendrath had close contacts with his relatives in Dorsten and also later on in Chicago, USA. His brother, Moises Samson Eisendrath from Dorsten, was present as a witness at the birth of his second daughter Brunette Eisendrath on 15 March 1846. In 1863 the two eldest daughters emigrated from Dorsten to the U.S. with their uncle Benjamin Eisendrath. In 1868 Marianne returned to the Netherlands, married Bernard de Jong and died just two years later in 1870.

In 1871 Bernard de Jong married Marianna's younger sister Sophia. Brunette stayed in the U.S. and married Henry Axmann. The sons Abraham and Henri stayed in Amsterdam, started families and were self-employed as booksellers. From 1867 one son, Nathan Eisendrath, lived here in Dorsten. The youngest son Samson started a family and ran a library in Gouda, Netherlands. The sons Moritz Baruch and Henri married two sisters, Henriette and Sophie Rosenthal from Dortmund-Hoerde.

Marriage Banns

It is hereby announced that the merchant MORITZ EISENDRATH of Amsterdam, son of the bookseller BARUCH SAMSON EISENDRATH and his wife EVA ABRAHAM née WITMANDT, both deceased, and SOPHIA ROSENTHAL, without profession, of Haerde, daughter of the merchant RAPHAEL ROSENTHAL and his wife CAROLINE née WEINBERG of Haerde, wish to enter into matrimony.
The banns were published at the local town hall on 16 May '83.
The Royal Prussian Registry Office
FELDMANN

Some of the grandchildren were also involved in the book trade. When they travelled round Europe, the American Eisendraths always visited their relatives in Amsterdam.

Mr and Mrs Berthold Eisendrath in 1925 in front of the shop in Amsterdam; on the right Joseph L. Eisendrath from Chicago.

On 9 February 1874 Baruch Eisendrath died while on a visit to Dorsten. His death was announced in the Amsterdam newspaper:

My dearly beloved husband, Mr B. Eisendrath, bookseller in this town, passed away today at his mother's house in Dorsten near Wesel at the age of 62. All those who knew the deceased during his hardworking life will understandwhatI,mychildren,theirspousesandhiselderlymotherhavelost. Widow B. Eisendrath, née Witmondt

The epitaph on his tombstone in Dorsten is:

Tomb
of a magnanimous man, he did good
and strove for justice
"the honourable" Baruch Eisendrath
and the name of his mother is Gitla [4]

---

4   Gitla instead of (see above) Güdla

'died the 22 of the month of Shevat
of the year 634" [5] *according to the shortened Hebrew year*
"May his soul be bound up in the bonds of eternal life."

Here rests
Baruch Eisendrath
Remembered by his children
And widow in Amsterdam
Born 8 July 1812
Died 22 Shevat 634 [5]

Eva Witmondt Eisendrath died in Amsterdam in 1880. 46 descendants of Baruch and Eva Eisendrath were deported from Rotterdam, Zaandam and Amsterdam and murdered. May their souls also be bound up in the bonds of eternal life.

Sources
City Archive, Dorsten
Archive of the Jewish Museum of Westphalia, Dorsten
Private Archives Family Eisendrath
R. Eisendrath: The effect of an urbun environement upo a large family group, Chicago, 1931

---

5   1874 (1240 + 634)

 # In Memory of the Family Members murdered in the Holocaust

At the Dorsten Jewish cemetery people who used to live in Dorsten are buried. Together with the many members of the Eisendrath family, let us remember those who are buried here and also all those who have no graves.

We recall and remember all the members of the family Eisendrath, especially those, who were deported and murdered from the family of Baruch Eisendrath:

Elisabeth Eisendrath, daughter of Abraham Eisendrath, at the age of 60 years, deported from Rotterdam, concentration camp Auschwitz

Marianne Eisendrath, daughter of Abraham Eisendrath, at the age of 71 years, concentration camp Sobibor

Frederika van der Linden, daughter of Marianne Eisendrath, at the age of 42 years, concentration camp Auschwitz

Barend Abraham, husband of Frederika van den Linden, at the age of 36 years, concentration camp Auschwitz

Hendrina van der Linden, daughter of Marianne Eisendrath, at the age of 36 years, concentration camp Sobibor

Nico Trijtel, husband of Hendrina van der Linden, at the age of 37 years, concentration camp Sobibor

Joseph van der Linden, son of Marianne Eisendrath, at the of 33 years, concentration camp Auschwitz

Sophie van der Linden, daughter of Marianne Eisendrath, at the age of 44 years, concentration camp Sobibor

Juda Trijtel, husband of Sophie van der Linden, at the age from 42 years, concentration camp Sobibor

The daughter, Maryon Sonja Trijtel, at the age of 8 years, concentration camp Sobibor

Albert van der Linden, son of Marianne Eisendrath, at the age of 39 years, concentration camp Mauthausen

Grietje Moscoviter, wife of Albert van der Linden, at the age of 44 years, concentration camp Auschwitz,

The children:
The son, Alfred van der Linden, at the age of 9 years, concentration camp Auschwitz

The son, Henri van der Linden, at the age of 7 years, concentration camp Auschwitz

Rebecca Klein, second wife of Bernard Eisendrath, at the age of 68 years, concentration camp Sobibor

Abraham Eisendrath, son of Bernard Eisendrath, at the age of 39 years, concentration camp Sobibor

Clara Presburg, wife of Abraham, at the age of 34 years, concentration camp Sobibor

And 3 childen
The daughter, Elisabeth Eisendrath, at the age of 8 years, concentration camp Sobibor

The son, Bernard Eisendrath, at the age of 5 years, concentration camp Sobibor,

The son, Henri Eisendrath, at the age of ½ year, concentration camp Sobibor

Sara Eisendrath, at the age of 67 years, died 1942 in Amsterdam

Hartog W. Lisser, husband of Sara Eisendrath, died 1942 in Amsterdam

Clara Lisser, daughter of Sara Eisendrath, at the age of 41 years, concentration camp Birkenau/Auschwitz

Salomon Nabarro, husband of Clara Lisser, at the age of 48 years, concentration camp Auschwitz

Sophia Lisser, daughter of Sara Lien Eisendrath, at the age of 33 years, concentration camp Sobibor

Abraham Willem von Sijes, husband of Sophia Lisser, at the age of 35 years, concentration camp Sobibor

The son, Eduard Hans van Sijes, at the age of 3 years, concentration camp Sobibor

Adelheid Eisendrath, daughter of Abraham Eisendrath, at the age of 63 years, concentration camp Auschwitz

Berthold Eisendrath, son of Moritz Baruch Eisendrath, at the age of 58 years, concentration camp Auschwitz

Sara Roosnek, wife of Berthold Eisendrath, at the age of 43 years, concentration camp Auschwitz

Henri Eisendrath, son of Moritz Baruch Eisendrath, at the age of 51 years, concentration camp Auschwitz

Eveline Eisendrath, daughter of Samson Eisendrath (NL), at the age of 56 years, concentration camp Auschwitz

Michael Levie, husband of Eveline Eisendrath, at the age of 58 years, concentration camp Auschwitz

Bernard Eisendrath, son of Samson Eisendrath (NL), at the age of 61 years in Amsterdam

Sortine Selma Juchenheim, wife of Bernard Eisendrath, at the age of 56 years, concentration camp Auschwitz

And the 4 children:
Iris Harriet Eisendrath, at the age of 27 years, concentration camp Auschwitz

Maja Frederika Eisendrath, at the age of 26 years, concentration camp Sobibor

Lydia (Leonie Emma) Eisendrath, at the age of 22 years, concentration camp

Rudolf Leonhard Eisendrath, at the age of 20 years, concentration camp Buchenwald

Rosette Eisendrath, daughter of Samson Eisendrath(NL),at the age of 59 years, concentration camp Auschwitz

Maurits Goldsteen, husband of Eva Eisendrath, at the age of 70 years, concentration camp Sobibor

Frieda Goldsteen, at the age of 29 years, died from gunshots in Amsterdam while running away from the Nazis

Isidore de Jong, at the age of 64 years, concentration camp Auschwitz

Jeanne Gros, wife from Isidore de Jong, at the age of 48 years, concentration camp Auschwitz

The 2 children:
The daughter, Jacqueline de Jong, at the age of 23 years, concentration camp Auschwitz

The daughter, Annie de Jong, at the age of 19 years, concentration camp Auschwitz

Diethard Aschoff
The Levi Eisendrath family in Laer

In the history of the Jews of Westphalia two facts make the Eisendrath family particularly significant; in the second half of the 19th century more members of the Eisendraths than any other family emigrated to America and in contrast to almost all the other Jewish emigrants to the U.S. of that period, we have been able to follow the development of this family. This is due to the fact that almost all the members of the clan who moved to America are descendants of Nathan Samson Eisendrath and those of his 18 children who survived; they settled in Chicago and today are still one of the strongest German-Jewish family groups with the motto "All for one and one for all"[1]. It is said that in 1933 the "Eisendrath Cousins Club" had 3000 members.[2] The close bonds between the members of the extended family are also reflected by the fact that the husbands of all Nathan Samson Eisendrath's daughters with their often large families emigrated to Chicago in the wake of the clan.

Another noteworthy point is the fact that the ties to their old home were never completely broken and the descendants developed a great interest in their genealogy; this may have to do with their unusual name about which American descendants speculated.[3] This interest led to initiatives regarding family history on both sides of the Atlantic and to family members meeting and being brought together.[4]

In this connection the story of Levi Eisendrath must be mentioned. He spent about one third of his life in Dorsten, one third in Laer and one third in Chicago. The most important period was without doubt the middle stage of his life between 1841/1842 and 1866 in Laer. From 1854 he was the head of the small Jewish community. It was here that he married three

1   Wolf Stegemann/S. Johanna Eichmann: Juden in Dorsten und in der Herrlichkeit Lembeck, Dorsten 1989, p. 248

2   ibid. p. 240

3   ibid. p. 242-243

4   Cf. in particular the book Stegemann/Eichmann, p. 204-209, with the family tree p. 214; p. 240-249

times, where his twelve children were born, where his first two wives and six of his children died.

On the history of the Jews in Laer before Levi Eisendrath came

In the prince bishop period before 1800, no Jews lived in the parish of Laer. On 21 June 1803 Isaak Jordan received a residence permit after paying a high sum of money. On 18 March 1818, the mayor Franz Heinrich Bauer[5] wrote, "Before this time no Jews had ever settled here."[6] Isaak Jordan was followed to this small place in 1808 by Isaak Levi Cohen, in 1811 by Abraham Baer and in 1812 by David Heimbach.[7]

The development in Dorsten was very similar where between 1808 and 1815 nine Jews settled including Samson Nathan, the father of Levi Eisendrath.[8]

In 1818 the Prussian government, which had been established in Westphalia since 1815, demanded that the mayors supply statistics on the Jews in their towns and villages. On 27 May 1818 the Jews in Laer consisted of four married couples, eleven children and one servant.[9] In 1812 there had only been 13 Jews in Laer.[10] All four families already owned properties of different but mostly low value[11], less than half of what average Jews in the district of Steinfurt owned.[12] On 10 June 1818,

---

5   See Klaus Schwinger: Laer/Holthausen. Geschichte der Gemeinde im 19. und frühen 20. Jahrhundert in: Schriften-
    reihe der Gemeinde Laer, volume 1, Laer 1988 p.10; born 1770 he was in office until 1838, ibid. p. 19

6   STAM Kreis Steinfurt LRA no. 136 fol. 29r *(r = recto, i.e. front)*

7   Diethard Aschoff und Gisela Möllenhoff: Fünf Generationen Juden in Laer. Leben und Schick-
    sal der Juden in einer westmünsterländischen Kleinstadt, Münster 2007 p. 7-8

8   Stegemann/Eichmann, cf. No.1, p. 52

9   STAM Kreis Steinfurt LRA no. 136 fol. 31v-32 *(v = verso, i.e. back)*

10 ibid. fol. 65v *(v = verso, i.e. back)*

11 ibid. fol. 66r; GA Laer A 257 fol. 15r *(r = recto, i.e. front)*

12 ibid. no. 136 fol. 86r. According to the sketch of the village of Laer with population register, in Schwinger, cf. No. 5,
    p. 10-17, no. 697, a garden, belonged to Isaak Jordan p. 11; no. 732, a house to Baer, p. 12; no. 739 a house to Da-
    vid Heimbach p. 12; no. 465 a garden to Abraham Baer p. 13; no. 777 a house to Isaac Levi p. 15

Mr. Bauer, the mayor wrote, "The trade carried out by the Jews here is not very significant and, apart from trade with livestock, has mainly to do with all sorts of things as it is mainly the case with Jews in rural areas."[13] Their financial circumstances were modest which is confirmed in a statement made by the mayor the same year when he said that, "The Jews do not have enough money to provide advances or make loans."[14]

According to information we have found, by 1835 the economic circumstances of the Jews had not improved. Here it says that Isaak Levi's assets were "quite low", Isaak Jordan's were "insignificant". Abrahm Baer's "quite insignificant, and David Heimbach's "very low".[15] This applied generally, of course. In 1831 Mayor Bauer wrote: "Due to the unfavourable circumstances that both farmers and craftsmen (mainly linen weavers) have had for several years, prosperity has decreased sharply and for most of the citizens it is really difficult to maintain subsistence."[16] In 1840 however, it was reported that in all four Jewish families "the financial circumstances improved in the past four years."[17]

How did Levi Eisendrath come to Laer?

At that time Laer obviously offered Jews a certain perspective. This seems to have been the reason why approx. one year later in around 1842, Levi Eisendrath, who had been born in Dorsten in 1818, moved to Laer. We do not know what Levi, who was then just 24 years old, did before that time. In 1840 in Dorsten, he was definitely not self-employed like his father and his brothers David and Moses.[18] The main reason for Levi's move to Laer was his marriage to Julia Sander née Cohen, a daughter of Isaak Levi (1776-1835)[19], who was the second Jew to move from Horstmar to

---

13   GA Laer A 257 fol. 144; STAM Kreis Steinfurt LRA 136 fol. 66r *(r = recto, i.e. front)*

14   STAM Kreis Steinfurt LRA, Nr. 136 fol. 30r *(r = recto, i.e. front)*

15   GA Laer A 259

16   Schwinger, cf. No. 5, p. 143

17   Aschoff/Möllenhoff, cf. No. 7, p. 23

18   cf. Stegemann/Eichmann, cf. No.1, p. 93

19   This must be the son of Levi Moyses mentioned in the lists of the Münster bishopric in Horstmar from 1763-1784.

Laer, and his wife Blümchen née Sander (1780-1853).[20]

The Jewish Community in Laer

The Jewish community in the village was very patriarchal. On 27 July 1843 the Mayor Adolph Steinmann[21] wrote to the District Administrator in Steinfurt: "The local Jewish congregation holds its services in a room on the upper floor of Abraham Baer's house," now no. 1 Hohe Strasse. "The congregation is not connected with any other congregation and is not prepared to be as there are ten males, i.e. the minyan, the minimum number of male Jews required for a service. The congregation has no assets and any expenses are shared equally by the four families. The present head of the congregation is the merchant Salomon Jordan who has been elected indefinitely and has no other function than responsibility for procuring the lights and other temple requirements. When matters concerning the congregation occur, they are discussed by the four family fathers."[22]

In Laer everything was organised pragmatically and without unnecessary expenditure which met with general approval. At funerals, the families helped each other bury the dead. In Laer this meant harmonious neighbourly relationships, comparable economic circumstances, modest and self-sufficient; it could almost be called an intact world.

A change for the better in the 1840s

In the 1840s things developed for the Jews of Laer: a synagogue was built, a cemetery was created and with the Prussian law of 23 July 1847 civil equality was extended to all Jews of Prussia and they were given certain political rights.

---

20 The Dorsten tradition, in the Laer archives and Detmold state archives there is no confirmation that in 1842 Levi married Angela Cohen and in 1843 Julia Cohen, Angela's sister. In Laer only the following children of Isaak Levi and Blümchen, née Sander, can be found: Angela, born on 12 September 1805 and Setchen, born on 4 March 1809, cf. Aschoff/Möllenhoff, cf. No. 7, p. 230. One possibility of explaining the discrepancy is that Setchen also used the name Julia. However, because of their age neither would have really been suitable for Levi Eisendrath who was born in 1818 and was thus much younger.

21 See Schwinger, cf. No. 5, p. 20-25 picture p. 21; born 1799, he was mayor from 1842-1844 and from 1844-1873 bailiff.

22 STAM Kreis Steinfurt LRA Nr. 136 fol. 177 r-v

The **synagogue** was built soon after 1843 in village no. 144, today Kamp 15. The two-storey building was approx. 85 sq.m. (915 sq.ft) in size and built on "a square floor plan" and had a hipped roof. The front was probably made of unplastered rubblestone. The triaxial building with simple lattice windows and an entrance door in the middle displayed no architectural features that indicated any sacral use. The 40 sq.m. (430.55 sq.ft) prayer room was at the back of the ground floor. The two-room apartment facing the street was let, the upper floor not converted into living space.[23]

Around 1845 the Jewish community bought a 365 sq.m. (3929 sq.ft) piece of land as a new **burial ground** at the Horstmar/Burgsteinfurt intersection. The registered owners were Baer Baer, who owned half the plot, Salomon Jordan and Moses Heimbach, who each owned one quarter.[24] Surprisingly Levi Eisendrath is not mentioned here although he already lived in Laer. The reason is unknown. But he did provide accommodation in his home for the old teacher Abraham Moses Schwalbach until the teacher's death on 27 April 1847 at the age of 81.[25] This is surprising because at that time Levi did not yet have children who had to attend school. This may suggest that also in his new, small-minded home village of Laer Levi Eisendrath, who had attended the Gymnasium Petrinum (high school) in Dorsten, was seeking a discussion partner well-versed in the Talmud.

The start of Levi Eisendrath's life in Laer
Levi Eisendrath must have come to Laer before 16 February 1842. That day he married Julie Cohen in Laer at a ceremony performed by Levy Michel of Recklinghausen.[26] He was a friend of the family and, as far as

---

23   Elfi Pracht-Jörns: Laer in: Jüdisches Kulturerbe in Nordrhein-Westfalen, part IV: Regierungs-
      bezirk Münster, Cologne 2002, p. 366-368, here p. 366-367, picture ibid. p. 417

24   Schwinger, cf. No.5, p. 155

25   GA Laer A 258 fol. 45r; ibid B 352 fol. 9v-10r

26   GA Laer B 352

we know, had been the mohel for all Levi Eisendrath's brothers.[27] Just like his eldest brother Baruch, Levi attended the Gymnasium Petrinum in Dorsten. His name can be found in the 1826 and 1830-1832 school registers.[28]

He was 23 years old when he got married and his wife, who was born on 19 August 1819[29], one year younger. At the ceremony, the bridegroom's parents were named as S[amson] N[athan] Eisendrath of Dorsten and his wife Julie Isaak; in the case of the bride's parents only Blümchen Cohen, née Sander, was named.[30] As mentioned, the father Isaak Levy Cohen, had died in 1835. When they got married the bride was already pregnant. The pregnancy may have been the reason for the „forbidden" marriage outside the residential district, as the Dorsten public authorities said. Moreover, Levi Michel, who conducted the ceremony, was not authorised to do so.[31] Isaak/Julius, the son Julia was expecting, was born on 10 June 1842 in Laer.

According to a list of the mayor's office in Laer, on 20 March 1843 four Jewish families lived in Laer; the butcher David Heimbach with seven persons in his household, the two traders Abraham Baer and Salomon Jordan with five resp. six persons and the merchant Levi Eisendrath with four persons.[32] As Nathanael Eisendrath, the second son, was not born until 14 July 1843, a maid[33] mentioned in 1845 may have been included in Levi Eisendrath's household.

Apart from births and deaths, very little is known about the life of the Eisendraths in Laer. We can mention that Isaak Eisendrath, born in 1842,

---

27   cf. STAD p. 8 no. 31 passim

28   Stegemann/Eichmann, cf. No. 1, p. 206

29   I can no longer trace where I found Julia Cohen's date of birth, cf. above note 20.

30   GA Laer B 352 fol. 5v-6r

31   GA Laer A 258 fol. 28r. Stegemann/Eichmann p. 244-245

32   GA Laer A 257 fol. 52r

33   GA Laer A 258

attended the 1848/1849 winter course and the 1849 summer course at the Christian school.[34]

Levi Eisendrath as head of the Jewish community and richest Jew in Laer

The Prussian law of 23 July 1847 mandated single Jewish communities in each city with compulsory membership of all the Jews living there under the supervision of the state. Together with the Jews in Rheine, Borghorst, Horstmar, Metelen and Ochtrup, the Jews of Laer formed part of the Burgsteinfurt synagogue district. The head of the community was extremely important. He was responsible for administration and order in the community and he supervised the officials of the community.[35]

On 21 February 1854, Levi Eisendrath was the only Jew from Laer to attend the elections for representatives of the Steinfurt synagogue district.[36] 38 people were present and he received fifteen votes, the eighth highest number, and was thus elected as the last of the representatives.[37] He accepted and this was confirmed by Steinfurt District Administrator von Basse.[38] On 17 August 1854 the three members of the board and nine representatives headed by Levi Eisendrath[39] met to discuss the statute of the synagogue district. According to records, "Mr Eisendrath was elected as leader and Mr Adolph Hoffmann of Neuenkirchen as recording clerk".[40] In this connection Levi Eisendrath was also elected head of the Laer synagogue community.[41]

---

34   Aschoff/Möllenhoff, cf. No. 7, p. 220

35   cf. ibid p. 33-34

36   STAM Regierungsbezirk Münster 17155 fol. 18r-22r

37   ibid. fol. 20r

38   ibid. fol. 22v

39   ibid. fol. 29r

40   ibid. fol. 29r

41   Ibid. fol. 38r

At first the statute consisted of 20 paragraphs but the final version of 3 September 1855 had 35 paragraphs.[42] Levi Eisendrath was the first of the representatives to sign.[43]

He was always the first to sign.[44] This applied to the first signature we have of 17 May 1843[45] when Levy had no official function in Laer. This may indicate that Levi Eisendrath enjoyed a special status in Laer.

Apart from the duties mentioned above, in 1854 as head of the Jewish community he was also responsible for collecting and allocating the money for the salary to be paid to Mr Sutro, the regional rabbi, which in Laer in 1854 amounted to 1 reichstaler, 16 silbergroschen and 9 pfennigs.[46]

In his community functions Levi Eisendrath obviously followed his father's example who in 1817 had been appointed head of the Dorsten community by the government, an office which he held until 1844.[47]

At that time Levi Eisendrath was the biggest Jewish taxpayer of the small community and, according to a list made by Mayor Steinmann on 22 February 1854, paid 6 reichstaler class tax *(a Prussian tax based on a person's social class or status)*.[48] At that time 17 Jewish people lived in Laer and his family accounted for six of them.[49] That year there were only eight Jewish children in Laer and fewer members than in 1818 when there had been 18 Jews in Laer. The descendants of Isaak Jordan and

---

42   ibid. fol. 29r-33r

43   ibid. fol. 55r-62v

44   cf. e.g. GA Laer A 258 fol. 34r

45   GA Laer A 257 fol. 51r

46   GA Laer B 352 fol. 38r

47   Stegemann/Eichmann, cf. No. 1, S. 107; 109

48   GA Laer B 352 fol. 36r

49   ibid. fol. 35r

Isaak Levi disappeared from Laer and with them the two oldest Jewish families of that place. The Eisendraths and Mildenbergs replaced them.

Many births

A new beginning came about and this, of course, had to do with the people living there. With established structures and laws to protect them, this was a flourishing period for the small Jewish community of Laer. Although we do not have any precise knowledge of the living conditions of the Jews in Laer, the large number of children, more than in the past and a number never reached again, does indicate that their financial circumstances were stable.

The five Jewish families living in Laer between 1850 and 1874 had a total of 50 children, i.e. on average, each family had ten children. This was also true of Levi Eisendrath.

Life and death in the family of Levi Eisendrath[50]

With his first wife Julia Cohen (1819-1845) Levi Eisendrath had two sons, Isaac/Julius born in 1842 and Nathanael born in 1843; with his second wife Emilie Löwenstein (1819-1852) he had three more children, Henriette 1846, Bertha 1849 and Calmann/Carl 1852 and with his third wife Helene Felsenthal (1826-1914) he had seven children in Laer: Nathan/Louis/Ludovicus born in 1853, Baruch/Bernard born in 1855, Oskar/Oscar born in 1857, Samson/Siegmund born in 1859, Emma born in 1862, Moritz born in 1863 and Max born in 1864. Five years later in Chicago they had one more child, a daughter named Ada.

So Levi Eisendrath had a total of 13 children from three wives. He had more children than any of his siblings and followed the example of his parents who had had 18 children.

---

50   Cf. Stegemann/Eichmann,cf. No. 1, passim, and the named archives

Records show that Levi's first two wives died very young, Julie at the age of 26 and Emilie at 33 years of age.

Infant mortality was high in those days and it took its toll[51] on all the Jewish families in Laer including Levi Eisendrath's. They lost

1. Nathanael Eisendrath on 7 December 1844, 9 months old
2. Henriette Eisendrath in the year of her birth, 1846
3. Calmann/Carl Eisendrath on 4 August 1852, 6 months old
4. Baruch/Bernard Eisendrath on 20 May 1863, not even 8 years old
5. Moritz Eisendrath on 20 February 1864, 3 months old
6. Max Eisendrath on 20 December 1864, not even 4 months old.

Thus death was no stranger to Levi Eisendrath's family. He lost two wives in Laer at an even then relatively young age as well as half the children born there, five of whom were still young babies. For his parents it had been the same. Of their eighteen children, six had died in infancy and childhood.[52]

Assimilation

The increasing assimilation of Jews, also in the rural areas of Westphalia, was also apparent in Levi Eisendrath's family just as in the other Jewish families in Laer: while he chose the traditional Jewish names of Isaac and Nathanael for his first two sons, only one of the seven following children had a name from the Old Testament, Samson, who was born in 1859. Three of the sons were registered with double names, Calman known as Carl, Nathan known as Louis and Baruch known as Bernard. Oscar, Emma, Max and Moritz all had non-biblical first names.[53] Apart from his synagogal name, Levi's oldest surviving son Isaac later also used the name Julius[54] as did Samson who later also used the name Siegmund. Assimilation also affected the religious sector. For example, in Dorsten,

---

51   Cf. Aschoff/Möllenhoff, cf. No. 7, p. 37-38

52   Philipp 1816; Marcus 1822; Semilia 1830; Philipp 1835 and the twins Bella and Rosa 1837, cf. Stegemann/Eichmann (see No.1) p. 214

53   Aschoff/Möllenhoff, cf. No. 7, p. 233, cf. p. 38-39

54   STAM Kreis Steinfurt LRA no. 220 fol. 47v

Levi Eisendrath's home community of Dorsten, law-abiding men spoke quite naturally of "church" instead of "synagogue" and "Easter" instead of "Pesach".[55]

Marriage partners

Levi Eisendrath also followed the custom of the Jews of Laer and married women from the Westphalian region probably, as was usual, with the help of a matchmaker. Levi Eisendrath's first wife, Julia Sander née Cohen, came from Laer, his second wife Emilie Löwenstein from Geseke in south-east Westphalia and his third wife, Helena Felsenthal, from Münster.[56]

Jews move away from Laer

Shortly after the foundation of the German Empire in 1871 the number of Jews in Laer decreased, many of them moving to other towns or emigrating. Apart from the bad economic situation, the main reason was that Laer offered no professional perspective.

One striking example is provided by Isidor Heimbach, a young butcher. In 1875 he moved to Münster and it was there that all his 13 children were born. When he died in 1927, children of his lived in many places including Hamburg, Bremen, Düsseldorf, Cologne, Hanover and Leipzig. Thus Jews moved beyond Münster to large towns in Germany.[57]

Emigration of Jews from Laer to America

From an economic point of view, the small places in the Münster region were not particularly attractive and emigration to the USA started in the 19th century. Heinemann Heimbach, for example, who was born on 5 June 1826, an uncle of the above-mentioned Isidor Heimbach, emigrated to the USA in the middle of the 19th century.[58]

---

55   Stegemann/Eichmann p. 89

56   Ibid., passim

57   Aschoff/Möllenhoff, cf. No. 7, p. 100-118

58   GA Laer A 257: pencilled note

Salomon Jordan, the eldest son of the first Jew to settle in Laer, also hoped for a better future on the American continent. He was born in Laer on 11 November 1808 and although, as already mentioned, he was the head of the community, in 1850 already aged 42, he left Laer together with his wife Lena, née Rose, whom he had married on 27 July 1842 and their four children.[59] Other Jews from Laer also emigrated, for example three members of the Mildenberg family went to Holland.

It was not only Jews from Laer, of course, who emigrated but, as everywhere in Westphalia[60] also a large number of Christians. Without claim to completeness, a list of emigrants from Laer/Holthausen who left between 1837 and 1900[61] shows 107 names, 12 of whom were Jews. They thus accounted for over 11% (11, 21%) of the emigrants. In 1858 Laer had 2299 inhabitants including 29 Jews[62], accounting thus for 1.26% of the population; this means that ten times more Jews than Christians from Laer emigrated.

Like other small places in the western part of the Münster region, the textile industry played a major role and Laer depended directly on the cotton from the southern states of the USA. During the American Civil War (1861-1865) the price of cotton yarn rose. Later the supply of yarn to Laer stopped completely.[63] The decrease in the number of inhabitants was due to the fact that cotton weaving stopped almost completely.[64]

Of the 107 people who emigrated from Laer, 89 went to the USA, i.e. 83%. Others went to South Africa (two), Brazil (two), Hungary (one), England (one) and twelve went to nearby Holland.[65]

---

59   Schwinger, cf. No. 5, p. 149

60   cf. for Dorsten and surroundings Stegemann/Eichmann p. 244

61   Schwinger, cf. No. 5, p. 149-150

62   Aschoff/Möllenhoff, cf. No. 7, p. 43

63   Schwinger, cf. No. 5, p. 83-84

64   ibid. p. 143

65   ibid. p. 144-150

Emigrants from Laer had to apply to the local authorities for an emigration permit and a passport. Their attention was drawn almost threateningly to the consequences: "Applicants were told to note the instructions and warnings particularly the fact that upon issue of the papers they would lose the right to demand to become Prussian subjects again if for any reason it was considered doubtful and that persons who may try to return in an impoverished state are to be refused admission at the border and if they nevertheless try to enter the country illegally, they should be treated as foreign vagrants."[66]

Many people did, however, disappear without permission and secretly either to avoid the hard military service or criminal prosecution.[67] This also applies to Levi Eisendrath and his brother David who was two years older.[68]

The end of the Eisendraths in Laer

This also included Levi Eisendrath who had first moved from Dorsten to Laer. According to the Laer emigration lists, he and his son Isaak left in 1866 to go to the USA.[69] The time was good, the American Civil War had just ended.

We learnt of their emigration rather by chance through the purchase of a property by the town. The story goes back to 1843. On 21 August 1843 Mayor Steinmann asked the District Administrator von Basse for permission to buy a garden from Salomon Jordan in order to extend the churchyard. For reasons unknown to us the purchase was never made despite the fact that a permit[70] was issued.

---

66   ibid. p. 144

67   ibid. p. 145

68   cf. Stegemann/Eichmann, cf. No. 1, p. 206

69   Schwinger, cf. No. 5, p. 148

70   STAM Kreis Steinfurt LRA no. 220 fol. 29r

The next we hear is on 29 December 1874.[71] At that time Levi Eisendrath owned the garden and other property; they may have been in his possession since 9 February 1847. That day Levi's son Isaak/Julius was registered as (co-)owner.[72] Records show that "the owner, a Jewish trader by the name of Eisendrath, accused of forging a bill, fled to America several years ago".[73] Since several members of the Dorsten Eisendraths had emigrated to America before 1850, the way there had already been prepared for Levi and his son Isaak/Julius.

Without their breadwinner, it seems the family could not stay on in Laer particularly as bankruptcy proceedings had been started and creditors were making threats.[74] In this difficult situation Helena Eisendrath understandably sought refuge at the "family headquarters" in Dorsten. On 19 July 1866 she received permission from the Laer bailiff to move to Dorsten.[75] Now the family group went into action again. In an amazingly short time the Eisendraths on either side of the Atlantic managed to organize the emigration of the Laer relatives to Chicago, to get the papers and money they needed for the journey and arrange for six members of the family to cross the Atlantic as safely and comfortably as possible. The fact that this was done in less than three months after they moved from Laer must be seen as an amazing achievement by the Eisendraths on both sides of the Atlantic. On 11 October 1866 Helena Eisendrath arrived in New York on board the "Hansa" with the five children, two from her husband's first two marriages and three of her own.[76] Her husband may have met them there and taken them to Chicago.

---

71   ibid. fol. 404-42r

72   ibid. fol. 54r

73   STAM Kreis Steinfurt LRA no. 220 fol 40r-42r. Mentioned in Peter Ilisch
      without name: Die Pfarrgemeinde St. Bartholomäus in Laer, Laer 1985, p. 150

74   STAM Kreis Steinfurt LRA no. 220 fol 40r-42r

75   Stegemann/Eichmann, cf. No. 1, p. 245

76   „Levy Eisendrath Genealogie", available at the Jewish Museum Dorsten, p. 1

Winding up the property of the Eisendraths in Laer

It turned out that Levi Eisendrath did not only own the plot bordering on the cemetery but also four more gardens as well as a residential and commercial building[77], thus quite a lot of property. According to a letter of the Burgsteinfurt land registry of 28 March 1876, on 9 February 1874 half of this property had been entered in the Laer land registry volume 67, sheet 80 under Isaak's name.[78] The relatively large property ownership of the Eisendraths in the village after less than one generation seems remarkable and indicates that in 1866 the family's financial circumstances were good.

In the above-mentioned letter of 29 December 1874, Hermann Jakob Bach[79], the Laer bailiff, wrote to the District Administrator in Steinfurt that in the summer of that year credtors of Levi Eisendrath "put up for public sale the property of said person located here including the plot bordering on the churchyard".[80] A sketch with the location of the garden is in the file.[81]

On 13 June 1878 the Laer bailiff August von Oy[82] asked the government in Münster by way of the Steinfurt District Administrator for permission to purchase the garden property of Isaac/Julius Eisendrath for 720 marks.[83] According to the Steinfurt land registry, on 30 August 1878 the municipality of Laer was the sole owner of the property.[84] Thus after less than 50 years the last connection of the Eisendrath family to Laer was cut.

---

77   STAM Kreis Steinfurt, LRA no. 220 fol. 45r-v

78   STAM Kreis Steinfurt, LRA no. 220 fol. 54r cf. ibid. fol. 68r, where on 30 August 1878 only the municipality of Laer appears as the owner.

79   See Schwinger, cf. No. 5, p. 25-26

80   STAM Kreis Steinfurt LRA no. 220 fol. 40r-42r

81   STAM Kreis Steinfurt LRA no. 220 fol. 55r

82   See Schwinger, cf. No. 5, p. 26-31, picture p. 27

83   STAM Kreis Steinfurt LRA no. 220 fol. 50r-v; 53r-v (copy)

84   STAM Kreis Steinfurt LRA no. 220 fol. 68r

Local records verify that Levi Eisendrath and his family were in Laer from 1841/42 to 1866, i.e. some 25 years. In some way for him Laer was just the stop between Dorsten and the USA. It was without doubt the accusation of forging the bill that led him to leave the place at the age of 48, the place where he had married three times and lost two wives who had borne him 12 children, six of whom he had had to bury mainly as babies and where he had been a merchant for 25 years and head of the Jewish community for a long time.

Levi Eisendrath in Chicago

We learn about Levi's years in Chicago mainly from Ruth Eisendraht's Master's thesis presented in 1931. It states that his profession in the USA is grain merchant even if he first worked in the liqueur business. Chicago is where his youngest child, his daughter Ada, was born on 5 April 1869.[85]

Levi was regarded as the "most sophisticated, best educated and most elegant" of the brothers, as the only example of the family who was struck by "tragedy and misfortune" due to "earlier and extremely unfortunate circumstances."[86] It is unlikely that this refers to Levi fleeing from Laer because of bill forgery in 1866 because Ruth Eisendrath did not even know that Levi had lived in Laer for twenty-five years. It is more likely that she is referring to the early death of his first two wives and the loss of six of his 12 children born in Laer even if he did not speak about this at all or if he did, then only very rarely. Otherwise the story would have been passed down through the generations.

While Levi's excellent education and his exemplary devoutness mean that he still enjoys a positive reputation in the family, Levi's third wife Helena, known as "Lenchen", left a terrible image in the family group. According to family legend she was only a good wife to her husband for as long as he was successful in his work. It is said that she never behaved in a friendly or motherly way to her two stepchildren Julius and Bertha, that she even rejected them that much that they turned away

---

85   Cf. Stegemann/Eichmann, cf. No. 1

86   Ruth Minna Eisendrath: The Effect of an Urban Environment upon a large Family Group, (unprinted) thesis, Chicago/Illinois 1931, p. 39

from their stepmother and sought sanctuary with other members of the extended family.[87] "Lenchen" is said to have only behaved in a motherly way towards her own children. "Everyone in the family was consciously or unconsciously aware of her ambition, her pride and her selfishness. She always insisted on living in the best area even if this meant that she was forced to take in lodgers."[88] In the memory of the family group she lives on as an extremely arrogant person. She basked in the glory she had gained by being the wife of a successful grain merchant. But when fortune abandoned her husband, she refused any further co-operation with him and made his life hell as the words, "She succeeded in making his life most miserable," suggest.[89]

It may well have been these circumstances which led to Levi Eisendrath increasingly seeking sanctuary in religion. As already mentioned, he had already played a role in the Laer community and also had an old Jewish teacher living in his house, no doubt also in order to be able to talk about religion. He was obviously also in close contact with the strictly orthodox regional Rabbi Abraham Sutro[90] for whom in Laer he not only collected the salary to be paid but it was also Rabbi Sutro who conducted the wedding ceremony in Münster when Levi Eisendrath married for the third time. In Chicago Levi Eisendrath was the Director and for many years also the President of the Kehilath Anshe Mayri[91] and was regarded as the most religious of his brothers and sisters in America. It was known that every Friday morning he put on the tefillin, the small black boxes with black straps, and read the Talmud.[92] It was typical of him, according to family legend, that in 1882 he was late preparing his last Seder evening and Pessach and in the haste he accidentally kicked the reins of his two-seater cart, the horse bolted and he was run over by the cart. He was not

---

87   ibid. p. 93

88   ibid. p. 95

89   ibid. p. 39

90   cf. Diethard Aschoff: Abraham Sutro, in : Biographisch-Bibliographisches Kirchenlexikon, volume 11, 1996, p. 283-287

91   Eisendrath, cf. No. 86, p. 247

92   ibid. p. 280

able to attend the Seder evening but insisted that it be celebrated without him. Shortly afterwards he lost consciousness and died.[93]

Helena Felsenthal – an attempt to save her honour

Levi's wife Helena, who was so unpopular in the family, survived her husband by 32 years. She did not die until 18 March 1914. Ruth Eisendrath's Master's thesis on the large family group probably did her an injustice. She does not know that Helena Felsenthal bore her husband eight children, three of whom died within 18 months of each other in 1863/64, Moritz and Max as babies and Baruch/Barnard at the age of almost eight.[94] We can hardly imagine what the loss of three sons in such a short time meant for the mother. Fate dealt another hard blow just two years later when her husband was accused of bill fraud and then fled to America. There she was with five young children without her husband even if the Eisendrath family group, as described above, helped. The loss of respect in the small place must have been terrible as well as the shame which her husband's offence and his escape to America must have caused, not to mention the financial consequences. Creditors probably made threats.[95] Here too the Dorsten relatives probably helped. The statement of the Laer bailiff of 19 July 1866 says that she „and her family, who are not able to work, have so far made a living with no support from public means" and have paid taxes up to 31 July of the year.[96] Despite the help she probably received from Dorsten, the responsibility for the five children remained mainly with her, also when she had wound up the household in Laer and moved to Dorsten. Nathan Eisendrath, Levy's brother, visited Germany in 1866.[97] He was the first Eisendrath to go to the U.S. in 1850 and his visit may have had to do with the emigration to

---

93   ibid. p. 250-251

94   Cf. Stegemann/Eichmann, cfl No. 1

95   STAM Kreis Steinfurt LRA no. 220 fol. 40r-42r

96   StA Dorsten

97   Eisendrath, cf. No. 86, p. 40

the U.S. of the Eisendraths from Laer. Despite all the support which the extended family gave them, the worry and care of the five children on the long and sometimes dangerous crossing in very cramped conditions remained with Helena Eisendrath. What she must have done for the family in the two and a half months between her move away from Laer and the arrival in New York is admirable.

According to family legend, she only offered her husband "a good, happy home"[98] in Germany, but turned away from him when, after a successful start, he suffered professional setbacks in Chicago. But three years after her arrival in the USA, the couple had their eighth child together when the mother was already 43 years old. Maybe, in view of what she had done for the family, Helena Felsenthal hoped for more recognition or expected that her husband might somehow compensate her in the New World for her work and the misery she had suffered as a result of his dishonesty and the consequences and she may have been disappointed that he did not manage this. In the tiny community of Laer, her husband was the head of the community and the richest Jew and as such he played a special role; it seems that this was also initially the case in the USA. The fact that this later changed may have alienated her from her husband in the latter years of their marriage. These thoughts are merely speculation as there are no sources to refer to.

Without doubt she suffered under the "stepmother syndrome": her two stepchildren Julius and Bertha, who thought that Helena rejected them and preferred her own children, suffered, as Ruth Eisendrath puts it, because they received no love[99]; whether this is correct or not, we do not know but they will not have spoken positively about "Lenchen". This view influenced the legend as did the reputation of the very devout Levi who determined the image of the couple despite the fact that he was not so successful professionally in the USA but maybe it was because he was born an Eisendrath.

---

98   ibid. p. 39

99   ibid. p. 39; 93

No memory of the Laer past in America

The memory of Laer seems to have completely vanished in Chicago. Everyone thought that Levi Eisendrath and his children had all lived in Dorsten. This is the only way to understand that Joseph Eisendrath said that he heard from his grandfather Louis Eisendrath, a son of Levi born in Laer, that he, Louis and his brother Siegmund were born in Dorsten and had lived their till he was 15.[100] Removing Laer from the family memory is part of the family legend which was built up in America and concentrated the whole German past of the extended family on Dorsten with a growing legend about the alleged 23 children of the ancestor Nathan Samson Eisendrath and his wife Julia Isaack who in the loving memory of the descendants was idealized as the perfect Jewish mama.[101]

Archive signatures used in the footnotes
GA: Gemeindearchiv (Community archives)
LRA: Landratsamt (District Council Office)
StA: Stadtarchiv (City archives)
STAD: Staatsarchiv Detmold (State archives Detmold)
STAM: Staatsarchiv Münster (State archives Münster)

---

100 Cf. Johanna Eichmann: Ein amerikanisches Familien-Imperium hat seine Wurzeln in Dorsten. Die Eisendrath-Story, in: Stegemann/Eichmann, cf. No. 1, p. 240

101 Cf. Johanna Eichmann: Sie war extravagant, wohltätig und auffallend schön. Julia Eisendrath – Porträt einer jüdischen Mamme, in: Stegemann/Eichmann p. 248-249

Tobias Brinkmann

German Jews in Nineteenth Century Chicago

In 1847, at the height of the last hunger crisis in central Europe, 24 year old Nathan Eisendrath packed his bags and emigrated to America, along with thousands of young men and women from his native Westphalia. Unlike Nathan Eisendrath almost all of these migrants were Christians. During the first half of the 19th century, very few Jews lived in Westphalia and other regions in northwestern Central Europe. For most residents of rural areas the prospects were dim. A growing population and the declining prospects in the rural economy explain why a growing number of people moved to the nearby cities of the Ruhr where they found employment in mining and the nascent iron and steel industry. Many Westphalians were also seeking a better future across the Atlantic.

After landing in New York Eisendrath spent a few years in Philadelphia and Pittsburgh where he found work in soap factories. In 1848, shortly after settling in Philadelphia, he married Helena Fellheimer, a Jewish immigrant from Bavaria. In 1852, he moved to Chicago, then a bustling and rapidly expanding city not far from the western frontier, finding employment as foreman in a soap factory. In the following year, having accumulated enough capital and knowledge, he launched his own soap production firm. The enterprise yielded funds for the investment (and partnership) in a small banking business. At the height of the Civil War, Eisendrath switched into the liquor trade and the grocery business. During the war Chicago became a major distribution and production center for the Union troops, and many businesses benefited enormously. Already by the end of the war Eisendrath was a wealthy man. A credit-rating firm estimated he was easily worth $100,000 (a sum that corresponds to c. $1,4 million in 2011). At this time, Eisendrath and his wife were raising four sons (Benjamin Washington, born in 1852; William Nathan, 1853; Abraham Nathan, 1855; Joseph Nathan 1859). A fifth son, Daniel Nathan, was born in 1867.

Eisendrath was one of the prominent members of the small Jewish community in Chicago. During his first decade in the city Eisendrath belonged to Chicago's first Jewish congregation KAM (Kehilath Anshe Maarab – Congregation of the Men of the West). In 1867 he was the leading founder of the North Side Hebrew Congregation (today Temple Sholom). Both congregations identified with the mainstream Reform movement in the 1870s. In 1874/75 Eisendrath served as president of United Hebrew Relief Association and thus was the symbolic leader of the Chicago Jewish community. While most contemporary records indicate that Eisendrath retired around 1870, he apparently continued to pursue various business ventures in and beyond Chicago. In the early 1880s we find him in the mining town Leadville, Colorado. According to the 1880 census taker he was a money broker. Eisendrath also secured the permission for a mining operation near Leadville in 1882. By the late 1880s he was back in Chicago. Nathan Eisendrath died in 1902, when he was 79 years old.[1]

Nathan Eisendrath was part of a Jewish migration wave from Central and Eastern European villages to the United States. Jews formed a small but distinctive part of a huge migration that brought 5.5 million German-speaking immigrants to North America between 1815 and 1914. The uneven Jewish Emancipation policies of the German states functioned as a specific push factor: discriminatory laws that prevented Jews from owning land, taking public office, and choosing certain occupations were only gradually lifted after 1815 and sometimes re-imposed. The notorious Bavarian "Matrikel-Law" of 1813, for instance, fixed the number of Jewish households in a given village or town at 1813-levels, thus forcing young Jewish men and women to seek their fortunes elsewhere. While the majority of rural Jews moved to large cities like Berlin, Frankfurt, Breslau, Munich and Hamburg, considerable groups left for the New

---

1   *Chicago und sein Deutschthum* (Cleveland: German-American Biographical Publishing Company, 1901/02), 496; Her-

man Eliassof and Emil G. Hirsch, „The Jews of Illinois: Their Religious and Civic Life, their Charity and Industry, their Pa-

triotism and Loyalty to American Institutions, from their earliest settlement in the State unto present time," *Reform Advocate*

(Chicago), May 4, 1901, 317; US Census 1880; Leadville, Lake, Colorado; Roll: 91; Family History Film: 1254091; Page: 363A;

Enumeration District: 78; Image: 0327; *The Engineering and Mining Journal* (New York), September 9, 1882, 140.

World. All Jews in Germany were fully emancipated only in 1871 when Imperial Germany was founded. Jews in the United States enjoyed full civil equality since the American Revolution. Recent research has shown the impact of socio-economic factors on the Jewish migration and close links to the large migration of non-Jews from the same regions to North America. Most Jews, like other migrants, established transatlantic networks: between 1840 and the early 1880s, for example, such a network "pulled" more than 100 Jewish men and women from a number of villages in the Palatinate west of Worms to the Chicago area.[2]

Most Jewish immigrants who came to America between the 1820s and 1870s originated in the South German states, especially in Bavaria, also in Baden, Württemberg and Hesse. Nathan Eisendrath's wife, Helena Fellheimer, was born in Augsburg. Another sizeable group hailed from the Prussian Duchy of Posen. Smaller groups came from Alsace, Bohemia and from several regions in Eastern Europe. Due to the separation of religion and state in the United States Jewish migrants were not counted as Jews but as citizens of their respective home states, i.e. as migrants from Baden, Prussia, Austria, Russia and so on. Therefore estimates of the number of Jewish migrants to the US between 1820 and 1880 range widely from 100.000 to 200.000. The majority of these Jewish immigrants moved to large cities, initially along the Eastern seaboard, in particular to New York and Philadelphia where small Jewish communities already existed since early colonial times. Many Jews joined other German-speaking immigrants and headed west, often after spending a few months or even years on the East Coast just like Nathan Eisendrath. They established new communities in Cincinnati, Cleveland, St. Louis, Chicago, Milwaukee, San Francisco, and in many smaller towns during the 1830s and 1860s. Smaller groups also settled in the South: in Atlanta, Memphis, Natchez, and particularly in New Orleans. Detailed research for Chicago indicates that Jewish migrants often did not go straight from their home villages to the destination city

---

2   For background see the first chapter of: Tobias Brinkmann, *Sundays at Sinai: A Jewish Con-*

      gregation in Chicago (Chicago: University of Chicago Press, 2012).

but "stopped over" in rural towns in the Midwest where they started out as peddlers and small storeowners before moving to a bigger city.[3]

Origins and Development of the Chicago Jewish Community 1840–1870

Chicago was one of the leading urban centers of the European migration in the United States during the 19th century. The city's history illustrates the full impact of the dramatic social, demographic and economic change American society and economy underwent in the second half of the 19th century. Compared with other cities in the Midwest Chicago was a latecomer, but its growth was breathtaking. Within a few years it rose from a small settlement along the frontier to the dominant "Metropolis" of the American continent. Chicago's booming economy attracted hundreds of thousands of immigrants from Europe and internal migrants from the American Northeast. Between 1880 and 1890 alone, Chicago's population doubled from 500,000 to over one million, making Chicago the second-largest city in the United States and the fifth largest in the world. Between 1890 and 1900 almost 80% of Chicago's inhabitants were foreign-born or children of immigrants. Even for the United States this was an unusually high proportion. The rise of Chicago went hand in hand with a growing degree of social disorder. Mass-immigration and rapid social change, accompanied by several economic recessions, caused social unrest. During the last third of the 19th Century Chicago became the site of America's worst outbursts of urban violence.[4]

Chicago's rise depended on three connected factors: location, the expectations of investors, and mass immigration. Between the 1850s and 1870s, the city emerged as strategically located traffic hub exactly between the seemingly unlimited raw materials and agricultural products

---

3   William Cronon, *Nature's Metropolis: Chicago and the Great West* (New York: Norton, 1991); Witold Rybczyn-

ski, *City Life: Urban Expectations in a New World* (New York: Scribner, 1995), 110–115; Avraham Barkai, *Branch-*

ing Out: German-Jewish Immigration to the United States 1820–1914 (New York: Holmes & Meier 1994).

4   Thomas L. Philpott, *The Slum and the Ghetto: Neighborhood Deterioration and Middle-Class Reform, Chicago 1880–1930*

(New York: Oxford University Press, 1978), 8; Carl Smith, *Urban Disorder and the Shape of Belief: the Great Chi-*

cago Fire, the Haymarket Bomb and the Model Town of Pullman (Chicago: University of Chicago Press, 1995).

of the "West" – in particular, lumber, grain, and meat which were processed in Chicago – and the markets on the East coast and beyond. The Civil War proved a catalyst driving the rise of Chicago against its main rivals, the river cities Cincinnati and St. Louis. Both cities were too close to the military action and suffered from trade blockades caused by the war. Chicago became the main production and supply center for the Union troops West of the Alleghenies. After the war, Chicago developed into the leading railroad hub of the American continent and a strongly expanding industrial center. While the processing industries, such as meat packing gradually began to move west before the turn of the century, Chicago remained a distribution center with an innovative service sector and, more importantly, the financial marketplace where the commodity prices were fixed.[5]

Chicago became a city in 1837. Only a few years later, in the early 1840s, the first Jews settled in Chicago, but often not for long. For several years there were not enough Jewish men to form a *minyan*, the required minimum number of ten Jewish adult men to hold a service. But already in 1846 the early settlers founded the "Jewish Burial Ground Society" which bought land for a Jewish cemetery from the city.[6] Setting up an institution comparable to the European *Gemeinde* was hardly an option in the United States. Before the Emancipation, the Jewish *Gemeinde* or *Kehila* in Central and Eastern Europe was an autonomous body, which served not just religious needs; it collected taxes and had a limited legal authority. The *Gemeinde* also provided for education and a number of social tasks ranging from caring for poor Jews to sick-care. With the Emancipation the autonomy of the *Gemeinde* was gradually curtailed, but the institution remained intact as the religious and social center of the Jewish community. In the German states all Jews were obliged to be members of the *Gemeinde*, which continued to be regulated and controlled

---

5   Cronon, *Nature's Metropolis*.

6   Illinois State Archive (Chicago), Chicago City Council Proceedings, 4 March 1846, Doc. No.
     3040: „petition of Israelites for purchase of Land for burial purposes".

by the state and would in larger cities comprise several synagogues, one or more cemeteries, and a variety of social services including schools.[7]

While in Europe the state defined and regulated Jewish communities even after the Emancipation, American Jews had (and have) to define, build and sustain Jewish communities on their own. The new American republic did not formally emancipate Jews; Jews were free and equal American citizens like all other (white) Americans. European Jews who migrated to the United States thus literally emancipated themselves by crossing the Atlantic.[8] The American Constitution of 1789 and especially the First Amendment of 1791 also guaranteed that nobody could be forced by the state to belong to a religious group; that the state did not intervene in religious affairs, and that membership in a religious congregation as in any secular association was strictly voluntary.[9] American Jews did not immediately feel the impact of state neutrality in religious matters. Before 1820 they were a small and quite cohesive group, most Jews belonged to the one congregation at a given place. But with increasing numbers of immigrants arriving, the existing congregations could not cope. The immigrants brought different cultural baggage with them during a time when especially Jews in Germany questioned traditional Judaism and developed concepts of modern Judaism. Already by the 1830s the first urban congregations split, while new immigrants founded their own congregations. Jews also founded secular Jewish associations, of which some, notably burial societies, collective relief-societies and sewing-associations had strong roots in the traditional Central European *Gemeinde*, while others like fraternal lodges and literary societies for young men and women were genuinely new.

---

7   Steven M. Lowenstein, Die Gemeinde, in: Michael A. Meyer (ed.), *Deutsch-jüdische Ge-schichte in der Neuzeit* (Munich: C.H. Beck, 1996), Vol. 3, 123–129.

8   Ira Katznelson, Between Separation and Disappearance: American Jews on the Margins of American Liberalism, in: idem/Pierre Birnbaum (ed.), *Paths of Emancipation: Jews, States and Citizenship* (Princeton: Princeton University Press 1995), 170.

9   Seymour Martin Lipset, A Unique People in an Exceptional Country, in idem (ed.), *American Pluralism and the Jewish Community* (New Brunswick: Transaction 1989), 9. The separation of religion and state in the American Constitution owes its existence of enlightenment-ideas rather than lobbying by religious minorities, see: Jonathan Sarna, „The Impact of the American Revolution on American Jews," in: *Modern Judaism* 1 (1981), 149-160.

Even before the middle of the 19th Century it was apparent, that especially in large cities with sizeable Jewish populations like New York, Philadelphia, Cincinnati and Baltimore new ways for organizing most Jews under one roof had to be devised. In Central Europe, especially in expanding cities such as Berlin or Hamburg, Jewish *Gemeinden* also faced tremendous social change, but the institutional framework as such remained intact.[10] In the United States, Jewish elites, hierarchies, or traditional institutions did not exist and the state did not regulate or control religious bodies. Therefore grass root community-building on the local level in the second half of the 19th Century provided the basis for national Jewish organizations and thus for the emergence of an American-Jewish ethnicity.

In 1847, several Jewish "pioneers" from the Palatinate and Franconia founded Chicago's first Jewish congregation, which they named appropriately *Kehilath Anshe Maarab* (Congregation of the Men of the West, KAM).[11] Only in its first four years, KAM resembled the traditional pre-modern Jewish *Gemeinde* most immigrants knew from their former home villages. Unlike the European *Gemeinde*, KAM would not serve the social needs of its members. In the early 1850s Chicago Jews founded several collective relief societies, which remained independent of KAM. And KAM, most of whose members hailed from South Germany, refused membership to Jewish immigrants from the Duchy of Posen who consequently founded their separate "Polish" congregation, *B'nai Sholom* (Sons of Peace) in 1851.[12]

It was not only *landsmanshaft* – affiliation to other immigrants from the place or region of origin – that divided Jews in Chicago. When Nathan Eisendrath came to Chicago in 1852 he encountered growing tensions within KAM congregation. In the 1850s, KAM (like many congregations in larger cities throughout the United States) was rocked by conflicts over

---

10   See for Hamburg: Rainer Liedtke, *Jewish Welfare in Hamburg and Manchester* (Oxford: Oxford University Press, 1998).

11   Hyman L. Meites, *History of the Jews of Chicago* (Chicago: Chicago Jewish Historical Society, 1924), 44.

12   Eliassof/Hirsch, Jews of Illinois, 299.

the introduction of religious reforms. In 1857, an outspoken reformer was elected president of KAM with two thirds of the votes cast. The traditional minority fiercely opposed any changes to the service and liturgy.[13]

Reform Judaism had emerged in Germany in the first half of the 19th Century as an attempt to define a platform for Judaism in the modern world. Reform was strongly influenced by the emergence of critical and rational *Wissenschaft* and by the German ideal of *Bildung*, which can be defined as constant spiritual self-education with a strong emphasis on universal principles such as freedom, equality, and openness.[14] The Chicago Reformers led by Bernhard Felsenthal aimed for a thorough modernization of Judaism along the lines of the German model. Felsenthal argued that external Reforms of the service did not make sense, unless Judaism was not redefined as a modern religion consistent with intellectual progress in the sciences and humanities. He considered Judaism as a progressive religion with monotheism being the core. Traditional religious practices that did not convey the essential religious truths were to be abandoned, new elements had to be added, especially a sermon in the German language because all congregants could understand it unlike many of the Hebrew prayers.[15]

In 1861, after several years of strife and conflict, the Reformers left KAM and formed their own congregation, "Sinai." The split coincided with the secession of the Southern states from the Union. The Cincinnati based *Israelite*, a Jewish weekly depicted the radical "German" Reformers in Chicago as 'rebels' who were about to 'torpedo the union'. "South Carolina is not alone to secede," declared the *Israelite* late in 1860, when the Reformers entered negotiations over the formal split from KAM. Nathan Eisendrath was not in favor of radical Reforms. He remained a

---

13   Meites, *History*, 63; *Israelite* (Cincinnati), October 16, 1857.

14   On the origins and the development of the Reform movement see: Michael Meyer, *Response to Moder-
     nity: A History of the Reform Movement in Judaism* (NewYork: Oxford University Press,1988).

15   Bernhard Felsenthal, *Kol Kore Bamidbar: Ueber jüdische Reform. Ein Wort an die Freunde derselben* (Chicago: Chas. Heß, 1859), 22-23.

member of KAM. But in 1867 he left, but not because he disagreed with KAM's turn to moderate Reforms. The North Side Hebrew Congregation, which he helped to establish in 1867, identified itself as a moderate Reform congregation just like KAM. The reason behind the founding of this congregation was not related to disagreements over reforms but had purely practical causes. The founders lived on Chicago's North Side, more than two miles away from the Near South Side where most Jews had settled in the 1850s and 1860s. Especially for the children it was too far to walk to KAM's school.[16] Nevertheless, the founding of several new congregations raised an important question: if Jews were to separate on the religious level, where was the basis for Jewish unity outside of the synagogue?

By 1861 it was clear not just in Chicago that unity for Jews in the United States would not be achieved within the synagogue. The rise of Reform partly explains, why Jews adopted the congregational (Protestant) model. It would, however, be too shortsighted, to explain the success of this model purely in religious terms.[17] Fights over reforms were also power-struggles over influence between groups and networks within congregations. Religious orientation, business-connections, social standing and not least *landsmanshaft*, created factions within congregations, and led to fights over influence.[18]

But where was the platform to bring Jews together beyond the religious level in America? One organization was trying to achieve this goal, the Independent Order of B'nai B'rith. This Jewish fraternal order, founded in October 1843 in New York, was the first secular Jewish association in North America.[19] The very act of founding the B'nai B'rith was an explicit response to the break-up of traditional Jewish *Gemeinde* that immigrants faced who came from rather traditional and closed Jewish

---

16   *Israelite*, November 30, 1860.

17   For a general overview see: Jonathan D. Sarna, *American Judaism: A History* (New Haven: Yale University Press, 2004).

18   Brinkmann, *Sundays at Sinai*

19   Deborah Dash Moore, *B'nai B'rith and the Challenge of Ethnic Leadership* (Albany: SUNY Press, 1981), 7.

communities in Central and Eastern Europe. Especially different regions of origin of Jewish immigrants and henceforth cultural and social differences between established and newly arriving immigrants constituted a serious problem for Jewish communities in the making.[20] And there were also political differences. In Chicago several known Jews joined other German-speaking immigrants as founders of the local Republican Party. Yet several Jews also represented German wards as Democratic aldermen in the Chicago City-Council as early as 1856.[21]

The B'nai B'rith was secular – but not anti-religious. Yet, religion, a potential source of conflict, was "off limits" for the brethren of the Order B'nai B'rith. The very same Reformers who eventually would split from KAM established Chicago's first B'nai B'rith lodge "Ramah" in 1857. But within the B'nai B'rith-lodge the Reformers worked indeed together with their opponents as "brothers" for the establishment of an institutional network, which would tie most Jewish congregations and associations in Chicago together.[22] The decisive step in this direction was the founding of the United Hebrew Relief Association (UHRA) in 1859. The UHRA was more than an organization devoted to supporting poor Jews, it represented the Jewish community of Chicago. All Jewish congregations, the B'nai B'rith lodge, and the collective relief-societies, became corporate members of the UHRA. The member-societies sent representatives to the annual council, which in turn elected the board. The UHRA was supra-religious and inclusive for all Jews. Like in other American cities overreaching organizations built on the traditional Jewish duty of *tzedakah* (social justice, philanthropy) provided the glue for binding diverse Jewish institutions together on a longterm-basis.[23] In a period when traditional Judaism came under intense pressure and when

20   *Allgemeine Zeitung des Judenthums* (Leipzig), July 27, 1846.

21   Alfred Theodore Andreas, History of Chicago (Chicago: A.T. Andreas, 1885), Vol. 2, 230.

22   *Report of the Eighth Annual General Convention of the Independent Order Bnai Brith* (Cincinnati 1859), 33.

23   *First Annual Report of the United Hebrew Relief Association of Chicago* (Chicago 1860). Tobias Brinkmann, 'Praise upon you:
     The U.H.R.A.!': Jewish Philanthropy and the Origins of the First Jewish Community in Chicago 1859-1900, in: Rhoda Rosen
     (ed.), *The Shaping of a Community: The Jewish Federation of Metropolitan Chicago* (Chicago: Spertus Press, 1999), 24-39.

the definition of Jewishness in a modern context became increasingly controversial among Jews, Reformers and traditional Jews, even members of secular Jewish associations, could accept communal philanthropy as a central element of their Jewishness. Jewish leaders emphasized that the UHRA was more than a charity-organization – it was *the* common platform for most Jews in Chicago. This background explains why the leaders of the UHRA, such as Nathan Eisendrath, who spent much of their precious spare time on behalf of Jews in need, belonged to the most respected Jews in the city.[24]

Jewish communities in other American cities were also organized on the basis of *tzedakah*. The UHRA and similar Jewish bodies in other cities were a Jewish response to the unique conditions in the United States, these philanthropic networks resembled an *Ersatzgemeinde*, which under the American circumstances had to be built and sustained from the bottom up and which had to be supra-religious. The UHRA and similar organizations were rooted in the Jewish tradition, but at the same time they served as institutional anchor of loose – compared with the framework of the German-Jewish *Gemeinde* – Jewish community-networks in the dynamic American urban context.[25]

Another important factor helps to explain, why private charity-networks assumed such a central role in the United States. Communal or state-funded charity was not available to the citizens of Chicago in the 19th Century. This forced in particular immigrants to form social networks to protect their members against poverty, sickness and other risks. Other immigrants in Chicago also organized overreaching benevolent associations, notably immigrants from Scandinavia, Eastern Europe and Germany. Privately organized philanthropic organizations, as immigrants founded them in the 1850s in Chicago, were in the historic process

---

24   *Allgemeine Zeitung des Judenthums*, January 12, 1864. The German original: „solange es Jehudim in Chicago gibt, mögen sie orthodox oder reformiert, deutsch oder polnisch oder sonst irgend etwas nennen. Hier ist der Boden, auf dem sie sich alle brüderlich vereinigen können".

25   Small town Jewry in America has hardly been researched, see: Lee Shai Weissbach, The Jewish Communities of the United States on the Eve of the Mass Migration, in *American Jewish History* 78 (1988), 79–108.

connecting chains. Communal philanthropy grew out of traditional forms of organizing social networks in European villages. In the American context these traditions assumed a new function by becoming the basis for overreaching ethnic communities and common identities. These common philanthropic organizations were formed as an institutional roof for earlier founded collective relief societies. To function at all, these loosely unified philanthropic organizations took a neutral position in terms of religion, politics and other potential intra-ethnic conflicts-fields. By organizing immigrants in this way organizations such as the UHRA promoted an ethnic-American identity, proving that the processes of becoming American and ethnic were closely related.[26]

Tzedakah, however, was not the only force that united Jews in Chicago. In the second year of the Civil War, B'nai B'rith-leaders organized a series of mass-meetings, which brought almost all Jews of Chicago for the first time together as a group. The first assembly voted to postpone all differences, explicitly the religious and political ones, for the duration of the war, in order to put up an all-Jewish company. $10.000 were raised and more than 100 Jewish volunteers formed a company – one of only two all-Jewish companies in the Union army – that fought in the war.[27] The company was part of a regiment of German-born soldiers, led by the famous Fourthyeighter Friedrich Hecker.[28] American patriotism also proved to be a unifying force for the loose community of Jewish immigrants, transcending all religious, regional, and other differences. Americanization and ethnicization were closely linked processes as the Jewish Civil War-meetings in Chicago clearly indicate. This experience was not limited to Jews. Other ethnicizing groups, in particular immigrants from Ireland and the German states also organized ethnic units. However, an important driving-force for the decisive action of the

---

26   Lawrence Fuchs, *The American Kaleidoscope: Race, Ethnicity, and the Civic Culture* (Hanover, NH: University Press of New England, 1990), 22; David Gerber, *The Making of an American Pluralism: Buffalo, New York 1825–60* (Urbana: University of Illinois Press, 1989).

27   *Illinois Staatszeitung* (Chicago), August 15, 1862.

28   For a more detailed account of the Jewish Civil War-effort see: *Illinois Staatszeitung*, August 14, 15 and 20 ,1862; *Sinai* (Philadelphia), September 1862, 231–233; *Chicago Tribune*, August 14 and 19, 1862; *Allgemeine Zeitung des Judenthums*, October 7, 1862.

Jews of Chicago in 1862 was the significant rise of anti-Jewish agitation during the war.[29]

The Chicago Jewish Community after 1870

Within a few years Jews in Chicago had created a united ethnic community, which impressed other ethnic groups in Chicago. During the Civil War German ethnic leaders praised the Jews of Chicago for their unity and called on the Germans to follow the Jewish example and overcome all differences.[30] But until 1870 Jews (unlike the Germans) were a relatively small group in Chicago. The developments after 1871 illustrate how urbanization and the strong growth of the Jewish population transformed the Jewish community. After 1871 the Jewish community of Chicago lost its momentum, but it did not disintegrate. Several factors explain the relative weakening of the Jewish community in Chicago, and in the other large American cities in the last third of the 19th century.

During the late 1870s Jews who had been born or grown up in the United States increasingly moved into the boards of congregations and associations. They had different expectations than the founders, which sometimes led to conflicts or growing alienation. Especially the large congregations, and not least the UHRA, struggled to attract younger Jews as members or donors in the 1870s and 1880s. Another factor was the expansion of Chicago. Although the notorious fire of 1871 destroyed its center, the city continued to grow.[31] Rapid urban growth led to increased residential mobility and thus more alienation. These developments presented a serious problem for the UHRA, as more and more Jews spread all over the expanding city.

The most important factor, however, was immigration. After 1870 Jewish immigration, increasingly but not exclusively from Eastern Europe, steadily increased. Almost all migrants moved to large cities,

---

29   On Grant's Order No. 11: Joakim Isaacs, Ulysses Grant and the Jews, in: *American Jewish Archives* 17 (1965), 3-16.

30   *Illinois Staatszeitung*, August 20, 1862.

31   Rybczynski, City Life, 115.

especially to New York, Philadelphia and Chicago. Existing Jewish relief-societies such as the UHRA supported needy immigrants but at the same time new immigrants were excluded from the associations and congregations of the established Jews, in many cases for decades. When Jewish immigration reached record numbers in the 1890s and soon after the turn of the century, with many immigrants in urgent need of support, the existing Jewish relief-societies were struggling. In several American cities, Jews from Eastern Europe, who like their predecessors were far from being a homogenous group, eventually founded their own "United" or "Federated" Jewish benevolence associations in the decades after 1880. The process described above repeated itself, congregations split, and immigrants founded an astounding number of associations, ranging from *landsmanshaftn* to Zionist lodges and Socialist trade unions. In 1913 Jewish immigrants from Eastern Europe in Chicago set up their own *tzedakah*-based community-network, the "Federated Orthodox Jewish Charities," which aspired just like the UHRA to connect the various Jewish congregations and associations, albeit on an explicitly religious platform.

For a limited period two organized Jewish community-networks did exist in Chicago. In 1923 the UHRA-successor organization merged with the "Federated Orthodox Jewish Charities", forming the "Jewish Charities of Chicago." But while the new body did represent the Chicago Jewish community, it was hardly comparable with the UHRA because of the large number of Jews living in Chicago. But Chicago's Jews differed to some extent from the other large immigrant groups, because they managed to sustain a strong sense of community.[32]

---

32   For the failed attempt to build an overreaching community which united established Jews and new immigrants in New York after 1900 see:

Arthur Goren, *New York Jews and the Quest for Community: The Kehilla Experiment 1908–1922* (New York: Columbia University Press, 1970).

Erik Schaap
The Eisendrath family in Zaandam

In 1942 and 1943 the German occupiers, helped by the Dutch police, expelled all Jews from the Netherlands, thus making it 'free of Jews' ('Judenrein', in German). The city of Zaandam was the first Dutch community where Jews were forced to leave their homes, as the first step in what the Nazi's called the 'final solution' (the 'Endlösung'). One of the many dozens of households that did not survive the Holocaust in that town was the Eisendrath family. You can see them on the first photo; father, mother and four children. I think this one was taken in 1927 or 1928.

Zaandam was a small town in 1940, with less than 40.000 inhabitants. 224 of them were Jewish. They had their own synagogue and their own cemetery, but were fully integrated into the local society. There was hardly any anti-semitism in Zaandam and the Jews, Catholics, Protestants and non-believers in this city all lived their lives, without religious or political problems.

from the left: Selma Juchenheim (from Vlotho), Sortine Selma Juchenheim-Eisendraht with the youngest Children

Bernard Eisendrath and his wife Selma arrived in Zaandam in 1914. Earlier that year they were married in Vlotho, Selma's native town. Bernard was born in Amsterdam. He became a doctor in 1907, when he was 25. He worked in several places as a military doctor before he moved to

Zaandam. As far as I know he had two reasons to settle in Zaandam. First of all it was two months before the beginning of the first World War and Zaandam had the biggest weapon factory in the Netherlands. At that moment there were about 8000 workers in that fast growing factory and the management needed a doctor for the workers. The second reason was that Bernard was able to get a good wage, a family doctor's practice and a beautiful house near the center of the city. You can still see this well-appointed residence on one of the photos.

While Belgium, Germany, Great-Britain, France and other countries were fighting during the first World War, the Netherlands succeeded in staying a neutral country. The factory Bernard was working for made a lot of money by selling arms to the battling countries, but the Netherlands itself stayed out of the war.

A year after they went to Zaandam Bernard and Selma 's first child Iris, was born. In 1917 they had a second daughter, Maja, and in 1921 the third, Leonie. Their last child was a boy, Rudolf, born in 1923.

All went well for the Eisendraths. It was a happy family. Bernard earned quite a lot of money and became a respected citizen. Selma was helping the local scouting and worked as a volunteer for a liberal party. Their children grew up and attended the local grammar school. The family always had one or two housekeepers.

Bernard Eisendrath was a well respected doctor, although sometimes a bit obstinate when he had to help his patients. I will give you one example. One of his patients, a schoolboy, suffered from migraine. He wrote: "My mother took me to several neurologists without any result. A doctor at the Amsterdam University Hospital declared that my eyesight was perfect and there was nothing wrong with my eyes to account for the affliction. I was really suffering when doctor Eisendrath insisted I come for an examination. 'The obvious problem', he said to my mother with great conviction, 'is that your son needs spectacles, never mind the expensive doctors.' He wrote out a prescription, which was promptly filled. I brought the glasses home, consigned them to a drawer in disgust, and never put them on my nose. I know that it must sound incredible as I relate this here, but believe me, I never again had a migraine in my life! My parents and I did not have the heart to tell the truth to the good doctor. Dr. Eisendrath went to his grave proud of his triumph over the university doctors. Thereafter he often liked to draw attention to my case, pointing out that 'science without intuition becomes impotent'."

The happy times did not continue. In 1933 Adolf Hitler became the absolute leader in Germany and soon after that the hunting of Jews began. As you know the Eisendraths had a lot of family in Germany and they heard their stories of persecution and anti-Semitism. The first sign I found that they were aware of the dangers was in 1934. In that year two Jewish German scouts left their country and found a shelter with the Eisendraths in Zaandam. Before World War 2 started both boys managed to escape to Argentina, as far as I know.

1936 Selma's brother and her mother also left Germany and went to the Netherlands. They became refugees. Selma's brother Paul and his wife went to Amsterdam, the capital of the Netherlands. Her mother Emma decided to stay with her daughter in Zaandam. At the beginning of 1939 another brother of Selma, Alwin, decided that it was no longer safe in Germany. He and his wife sent their son and daughter to Zaandam. They stayed there until December 1941. In that month their parents received the order to leave their homes. They had to report for work in Poland. Nowadays we know that working in Poland was the same as being taken to a concentration camp. But in those days almost nobody knew that the extermination camps were the last place on earth for the Jewish people in Western Europe.

Selma's brother and his wife were in doubt what to do with their children: leaving them in Holland or taking them on their own journey to another, unknown destination. They did choose for the second option and in the following years the whole family was killed in different concentration camps.

Let's go back to the Netherlands. On the 10th of May 1940 German troops invaded the Netherlands. It was a short battle. The Dutch troops did not have enough arms, war experience and soldiers to fight the Germans. It took only four days before the Dutch army surrendered. On the day the invasion started Dr. Eisendrath helped with the typhoid vaccinations that were being carried out in Zaandam – just as if it was a normal day.

In the beginning, the German invasion still had relatively few consequences for the Dutch Jews, although, after a month, son Rudolf was taken to prison for a day. Not because he was Jewish, but because he had used a stargazer to have a better look at a fire in the neighbourhood. For a short while the nazi's thought they had captured a spy.

Anti-Jewish measures were introduced step by step. It turned out in November 1940 that Jewish teachers were being dismissed. Members of the Board of Governors of the school visited by the Eisendrath children wanted to organize a protest strike. Rudolf Eisendrath was one of the organizers. But the members of the Board were summoned by the headmaster, who begged them to refrain from any activities whatsoever. Obeying him, the Board did not take action. The president of the Board at that time briefly mentions this event in a book he wrote sixty years later. He wrote: "With a little bit more tact the headmaster could have regarded our protest as a helpless attempt at showing our concern and sympathy. Instead of that, our boss was only afraid, afraid of the consequences of our protest. Now, sixty years later, this still hurts. One of the members of our little delegation was Rudolf Eisendrath, a Jewish classmate of ours. Why did our headmaster not embrace Rudolf´s shoulders and ours?"

From the 1st of September 1941 the children of the Eisendrath family were no longer welcome at their school. From the 1st of May 1941 Bernard Eisendrath was allowed to treat only Jewish patients. He had to sell his practice, but in spite of that still worked as a doctor. For example, he visited a patient who lived in a nearby street. Because she was Jewish, Bernard, as a precaution, climbed through a window of her house to get in.

As I said Zaandam was the first Dutch community where Jews were forced to leave their homes. When it was proclaimed on the 14th of January 1942 that the Jewish inhabitants of Zaandam had to gather in the Jewish quarter of Amsterdam, Bernard Eisendrath tried to sell several properties or to give them to someone for safe-keeping. The rest of their belongings were taken by the nazi's.

On 17th January a police-officer checked whether the Jewish inhabitants had left their homes. He also went to the doctor's family. As a foreigner, at first grandmother Emma Juchenheim was not allowed to go to Amsterdam. She had to leave for the concentration camp Westerbork, two days later. The duty-officer, however, came to the conclusion that she was seriously ill and so was allowed to stay in Zaandam for the time being. The officer wrote in his report: "Mrs Eisendrath was so distraught that shortly before leaving her house she broke down and was unconscious for some time."

This situation did not, of course, prevent the family from having to leave. The house was sealed, the door-keys collected. Shortly afterwards the occupying forces had the furniture that had been left in the house taken away.

Selma's 87-year-old mother was the oldest Jewish inhabitant forced to leave Zaandam. Due to her illness she got permission to go to Amsterdam instead of Westerbork. The Eisendrath family was able to find a flat in Amsterdam. Staying there, in poor circumstances, Bernard became so depressed about the new situation and the threats, that he committed suicide by taking poison. That happened on the 4th of October 1942.

I am not sure when Selma, her mother and her four children went underground, but it must have been shortly after the death of her husband. A friend of Selma who lived in Zaandam rented a flat for them in Amsterdam, probably at the beginning of 1943. Two months later Leonie Eisendrath met a classmate of Rudolf. He attended a nearby school. Leonie took him to her cover-address. There Rudolf lived with his other sisters and an aged lady, his grandmother. The room was bare and sparsely furnished: there were only some mattresses on the floor. The classmate came back several times, but at the end the family had disappeared and the room was empty.

Selma was the first one who had left Amsterdam. At the end of 1942 she was staying in the Israelite Old People´s Home in Arnhem, a city about 75 miles from Amsterdam. I suppose she went there to accompany her mother, who also lived there for a couple of months. Selma worked there as a nurse. The great majority of the elderly residents in this Old People's Home were murdered in the period between November 1942 and February 1943. Grandmother Juchenheim survived until April 1943, but was then deported to the concentration camp Westerbork. She stayed there for only three days. On the 16th of April – after a 72 hour journey in a closed cattle wagon – she was gassed in Sobibor, almost immediately after arriving there.

It was a horrifying week for the family. Earlier in my story I already mentioned Paul Juchenheim, Selma's brother. Paul and his wife had left Germany, because of the Hitler regime. Because his wife wasn't Jewish there was hardly any risk that he had to go to a concentration camp. Normally he would have survived the war. But on the day his mother, Emma, arrived in Westerbork, Paul was shot in Amsterdam. Three days earlier he dropped, by accident, a bag with some coal in it. It fell from the balcony of Paul's house and hit a German soldier. Paul apologized for the accident and it seemed as if the problem was solved. But three days later some German and Dutch policemen went to Paul's house, took him outside and shot him. It was their revenge for a simple accident. Mother and son Juchenheim were killed in the same week, in different ways and a different place, but for the same reason: they were Jewish.

A month after the death of her grandmother Iris Eisendrath was arrested. She did not wear a star of David and had false identity papers, but was recognized by a policeman who lived in Zaandam. He was a member of the so called Kolonne Henneicke, that had been specially set up to search for Jews. This policeman alone succeeded in finding more than 140 Jewish people. Most of them did not survive the Holocaust. After the war this policeman was to be condemned to death for his collaboration with the Nazi's. Later on the sentence was commuted to lifelong imprisonment. Just like her grandmother Iris was taken to Westerbork. But on the same day that she arrived there, she managed to escape from the camp. I don't know how she did that, but it was a true miracle. From the 100.000 Jewish people that were captured in Westerbork about 200 or 250 managed to escape. Iris was one of them. She went back to Amsterdam, where she found a new hiding place.

The deportation of grandmother Juchenheim, the arrest of Iris; caused panic in the family. The whole family fell apart. Selma was still working in Arnhem. Maja found a hiding-place near her mother's work. Iris stayed in Amsterdam and Leonie in Utrecht, another big city. Rudolf made a different decision. He decided to escape to Switzerland, a neutral country during World War 2. He succeeded in passing the borders of Belgium and France, but was arrested in Paris. He had false identity papers and was not recognized as being Jewish. Nevertheless he was sent to a German labour camp, Dora-Mittelbau. A great many of the prisoners there had to stay under the ground day and night and to work in the production of weapons. The mine galleries were called 'tunnels of death'. The circumstances in this camp were so hard that Rudolf died in less than two weeks, in march 1944. He was 21 years old.

As I said, Maja found a hiding place at a short distance from her mother. There she made a fatal mistake. She met a guy of her own age, a guy she knew from her time in Zaandam. Maja fell in love with him. He told her that he was working in the resistance, but in reality he was working for the Germans. Maja trusted him and told him where her sisters and, that is what I think, where her mother were living. One by one they were arrested. Maja was the first to be taken to Westerbork. She stayed there for only one night and then was deported to Sobibor, on the 6th July 1943 – separated from her mother and sisters. She was one of the last of the 71 inhabitants of Zaandam to be transported to Sobibor. Three days later she died in the gas chamber.

The next one who arrived in Westerbork was mother Selma, a week after Maja was deported to Sobibor. Selma was in a bad condition and therefore brought to the hospital in Westerbork. It's cynical, but in these days Westerbork had the best hospital in the Netherlands. There were a lot of doctors, nurses and all kind of specialists, all Jewish of course. In a letter to a friend Selma wrote: "For two days I have been taken outside the hospital for a few hours a day. A nurse helps me while I am trying to walk again." As soon as she felt a little better the camp staff judged that she was fit enough to be deported to Auschwitz. At the end of August she was killed.

One day after their mother was sent from Westerbork to Auschwitz Iris and Leonie arrived in Westerbork. Maja's 'friend' had found the two girls in their hiding places and he brought them to the Sicherheitsdienst, the German police in the Netherlands. They stayed in a prison in Amsterdam for a couple of days before they were taken to Westerbork. On the last day of August 1943, while in that camp, Iris wrote a letter of farewell to some friends. I quote: "By the way, Leonie and I have discovered during the past months that you can always and everywhere make something out of anything, that you are always able to derive some – however small – pleasure from something. In the cell in Amsterdam we had some pleasure, in the theatre – that was another prison – as well; you cannot imagine how much fun we still had even there."

In Westerbork they were taken to the 'Strafbaracke' – another cell, just a little more than 2 square metres. In her farewell letter Iris says: "This is probably the last opportunity of sending a sign of life to the outside world."

Iris and Leonie knew of their mothers deportation and hoped to see her 'there', although they did not know where 'there' was. They had no idea that their mother had been murdered three days earlier. Iris wrote: "Anyway, I am glad that Mother has not been in prison. I think father

113

was right, after all. (...) It was terrible, however, that she was sent to Auschwitz just one day before our arrival. Now we only hope to see her and Maja over there, but there is only very little hope."

Leonie wrote to her friends about the lack of warm clothes for 'Riga, or wherever we will go to'. She asked to say sorry to Mrs Van Meurs where she obviously had found a hiding place. "Of course I have said to the police that these people did not know anything about my identity. I hope this was sufficient and that they will not have any trouble about it." And later: "Will all of you enjoy your lives with all your might as long as you are able to do so? God knows what is still awaiting you."

In the meantime the two sisters were sure 'to be taken to the cattle wagon tomorrow, together with the other prisoners, to be locked up there again – under these circumstances I do not see any chance at all of escaping our destiny once more. Now, if there is no other way, we will go with a cheerful heart'. They were well aware that their future would be dark: "Working is not at all bad, you know, on the contrary, (...) but that you are not even granted the most simple human rights – that you are treated as nothing but cattle, or no, a proper farmer will care much more about his cattle than our 'protectors' do for us – that makes everything so wretched (...) It is nearly impossible for me to imagine that it was me who lived in Zaandam and enjoyed all the comfort and cosiness there."

Leonie also wrote: "When you cannot keep yourself decent, the world stops going round. (...) Furthermore, I see things quite soberly. We do not really stand a chance of surviving - but as fate will have it, so let it be (...). I am sure that lots of good and loving wishes will accompany us – and that will give us comfort." Iris and Leonie were sent to Auschwitz on the 31st of August 1943. They died in the gas chamber three days after their departure from Westerbork.

Rudolf was the last one to die, in 1944. With him the Eisendrath family tree in the Netherlands stopped. The only Eisendrath that survived the Holocaust was a sister of Bernard.

Helmut Drüing

The Kiäpenkiärl
i.e. the man with a basket on his back

Tonight, Kiepenkiärl welcomes all the guests here, but especially the guests from America from the bottom of this heart. In your program for tonight there is announced a "Westphalian evening" in this lovely location, the "Heimathaus" in Lippramsdorf. Typical Westphalian food will be offered. Members of the Museum association have invited us. And whenever "Westphalia" is the topic, one unique figure must not be missing, and that is me, the Kiepenkiärl!

Family reunion of the Eisendraths in Westphalia: It is unbelievable from which parts of the world you all come from! San Francisco, Ocean Side, Los Angeles, Chicago, New York, (Oh, difficult for me to speak) Massassuchets – all these places in America. In Europe, you come from Belgium which is just lying around the corner. Having you all here is a great honor for us.

Everybody who is here stems from one (pardon: two) person, because in 1810, 200 years ago, your grand-grand-grand-grand-grandfather, Nathan Eisendrath moved to this place, Haltern.

What I am aiming at? Well, deep in your heart, you all are of Westphalian origin. Don`t you feel it? You will certainly gain such a "Westphalian" feeling when listening to me:

First I am talking in my mother tongue "Plattdeutsch", which means the German dialect spoken in the flat Northern part of Germany. "Flat" means "Platt". Then I at once translate my "plattdütsche" words in English so that everybody can understand. Perhaps some of our guests can understand "Plattdeutsch", because it is similar to English and Dutch: Wat = what, dat = that, alleene = alone , dochter = daughter

115

Nathan Eisendrath has certainly spoken and understood "Plattdeutsch". When he moved to America, he has had no problem with the English language because of his good Plattdeutsch.

Let us now begin to talk about these two terms, these two big words which belong forever together: "Westphalia" and its "Kiepenkiärl".
In the old days, Kiepenkiärl was that man who was walking across the rural countryside between the so-called "Sauerland" in the South and Hamburg in the North and, above this, near and across the Dutch border. In short: Kiepenkiärl was the living connexion between city and countryside, between the people.

What have I done in the 17., 18. and 19. century? Well, with my basket I have collected food when I visited the farmers all over Westphalia, e.g. bread, butter, eggs, meat (ham), sausages, potatoes .. and Schnaps! That is our traditional Westphalian liquer, destilled out of wheat, and bottled by numerous distilleries in Westphalia. Alcohol: 32 or 38 % by volume. I think we have a break now because we will test it!

Whenever my "Kiepe" (i.e. the basket on my back) is empty, I always buy in return something back, e.g.: salt, sugar, perhaps a fine dress for the farmer`s wife.

In this way, I keep everybody satisfied … Do you know, what is typical of an original Westphalian? No? I tell you: Whenever he likes something he does not say: "This is good." Instead, an old Westphalian will always say: "This is not bad." So, an old Westphalian always prefers the indirect use of the words.

But the most important thing you cannot buy with money I bring back from the city to my rural customers: News! In my time there has not existed any newspaper in the country. Internet, TV, Radio did only exist in some dreams. Thus, I have been the storyteller:

Not long ago, there was a farmer coming up to me and asking me whether I could help him finding a wife for him "… if I knew some female in a similar situation waiting for a man". Kiepenkiärl would come around the country and would know where a wife could be found. The farmer could not leave his cows for a single day. At this point of the conversation I have to interfere insofar that you have to avoid the mistake saying at once "Yes" when you are in contact with a Westphalian. No! You have to leave him somewhat insecure. First he wants something from me, and second, to be in want of a wife is most of the time a highly sensitive matter. "Tja" is my first answer to the farmer. To be honest, I have to think hard about this matter. "Think carefully about it" says the farmer. And when you come back next time, I hope for a positive answer. "I will see what I can do" I reply. And by the way: If my effort in seeking a wife for you is successful, how does this (movement with the thumb) look like? "Oh", says the farmer. That is no problem. Then I fill your "Kiepe" once for free – as a token of goodwill. "What`s that?, I reply. That`s all you want to invest for a young wife on your farm? Oh.... I can think and think, but – honestly – I have no idea! I can´t help you!"

And now the story comes to its climax: What then followed has been the birth of your American currency. Why? Well, the farmer said to me: If you succeed in finding a good wife for me, you get ten "Daler" (= Dollar) from me! You see?

What Abraham has been to the Israelites, that has Samson Nathan Eisendrath been to his descendants sitting this evening at the Eisendrath family`s old place in Germany. Samson´s wife joined him one year later coming from Amsterdam. In 1812 she arrived here in Westphalia together with one child. In the following years they founded a very big family.

Samsons hobby was playing cards like many Westphalians do even today with "Skat" and "Doppelkopp". The legend goes that in some nights they played till the morning dew.

Samson Nathan was very much in favour of an open-minded hospitality. He always was fond of having his house full of guests. He always was friendly and liked to laugh. And! – He liked to drink a – right!- Schnaps!

I have to close now: But before I do this I have to tell you one special event: Some months ago, one out of the Eisendraths returned to Europe, to Dorsten. He met a farmer and told him about America and exaggerated: These huge houses, these gigantic land, and so on! The farmer remarked a donkey in front of him and chased him away with the words: "These Westphalian rabbits, they make me poor by eating all the grass around here…"

Kiepenkiärl segg (=says) "Danke" for listening to me and wishes the Eisendrath family, wishes you all a very fine and unforgettable stay here in Westphalia, the land of your forefathers. God bless you all!

Annex

Schedule of the reunion of the Eisendrath family in Dorsten, Germany
from 7 July to 11 July 2010

Wednesday, 7 July 2010
Arrival in Dorsten, Germany

Thursday, 8 July 2010

10:00 a.m.	Get together for all participants at the Jewish Museum of Westphalia in Dorsten Address: Julius-Ambrunn-Strasse 1, Dorsten
10:30 a.m.	Participants will be welcomed by the board of the Jewish Museum President: Norbert Reichling
11:00 a.m.	Presentation of programme of the Eisendrath Reunion Deputy President: Elisabeth Cosanne-Schulte-Huxel
11:15 a.m.	"From Dorsten to Chicago" Talk on the story of the Eisendraths Johanna Eichmann – Honorary President of the Museum / former principal of the Ursuline High School in Dorsten - Speaker: Laurence Browning
1:00 p.m.	Snack at the museum
2:00 p.m.	Tour of the museum and discussion led by Norbert Reichling (Director of the Jewish Museum)
3:00 p.m.	Coffee break with homemade cakes
4:00 p.m.	Germans, Jews or Americans? The Jewish Migration from Central Europe to Chicago, 1820-1900 Speaker: Tobias Brinkmann – Malvin and Lea Bank Associate Professor of Jewish Studies and History Department of History & Religious Studies, Penn State University/USA

| 6:00 p.m. | Press conference with local editors |
| 8:00 p.m. | Barbecue by the canal with members of the Museum Association – Address: Am Kanal 188, Marl |

Friday, 9 July 2010

9:00 a.m.	Participants meet at the Jewish Museum in Dorsten
9:15 a.m.	Description of the Eisendrath family on the basis of the genealogy scroll Speaker: Stefan Eisendrath from Lennik/Belgium
10:15 a.m.	Story of the Bernard Eisendrath family in Zaandam/ Netherlands Speaker: Erik Schaap from Zaandam/Netherlands
11:15 a.m.	Story of the Levi Eisendrath family in Laer/Münster Diethard Aschoff, Honorary Professor retd., Münster University – Speaker: Pat van den Brink
12:30 p.m.	"Altes Rathaus" (Old Town Hall) on the market place: Welcoming speech by the Mayor of Dorsten, Lambert Lütkenhorst Snack at the Altes Rathaus
2:00 p.m.	"Jewish life in a small Westphalian town two hundred years ago" Speaker: Josef Ulfkotte
2:30 p.m.	Walking tour of Dorsten – streets and houses where the Eisendraths once lived together with general information on the history of Dorsten organized by Information Office Dorsten/Jewish Museum (Barbara Seppi)
5:00 p.m.	Drive to the Jewish cemetery in Dorsten where the graves of Julia, Samson Nathan and Baruch Eisendrath will be visited
8:00 p.m.	"Westphalian evening" with typical Westphalian food at the Heimathaus Lippramsdorf (local history house) with members of the Museum Association and a „Kiepenkerl"

Saturday, 10 July 2010

until 10.45 a.m.	No official programme - time to visit the market or go shopping in the town centre of Dorsten
10:45 a.m.	Bus journey to Münster
12	noon Guided tour of the city of Münster incl. old town, cathedral, Prinzipalmarkt (main market square) Guide: Professor Martin Korda, German-American Society, Münster
2:00 p.m.	Peace Hall (where in 1648 the Peace of Westphalia Treaty was signed)
6:00.p.m.	Return by bus to the castle of Lembeck
7:00 p.m.	Photographs with all participants on the castle Lembeck steps – Address: Schloß Lembeck, Wulfener Strasse, Dorsten
7:30 p.m.	Dinner at Lembeck castle, Schlaunscher Saal (historical space) Welcoming speech from Ferdinand Count of Merveldt (owner of the castle)

Sunday, 11 July 2010

10:00 a.m.	Bus trip: Sightseeing tour of modern-day Dorsten accompanied by the Mayor of Dorsten, Lambert Lütkenhorst Tour includes former mines, industrial park, urban renewal
1:00 p.m.	End of the Tour Farewell at the Museum

List of participants

Eisendrath, Adam	San Franzisco/CA
Eisendrath, Stuart	San Franzisco/CA
Eisendrath, Alison. M.	Evanston/IL
Franchere, Joseph	Evanston/IL
Franchere, Evan	Evanston/IL
Franchere, Damian	Evanston/IL
Eisendrath, Aaron	Boston/Mass.
Eisendrath, Arpoo	Boston/Mass.
Eisendrath, Charles	Ann Arbor/MI
Eisendrath, Julia	Ann Arbor/MI
Eisendrath, Ben	Washington, D.C.
Eisendrath, Mark	Baltimore/MD
Eisendrath, David	Tarrytown/NY
Appel-Eisendrath, Patricia	Tarrytown/NY
Eisendrath, Edward	Greendale/Wisconsin
Eisendrath, Alice	Greendale/Wisconsin
Eisendrath, Edwin	Chicago/IL
Schulze, Jennifer	Chicago/IL
Eisendrath, Emma	Chicago/IL
Eisendrath, Jake	Chicago/IL
Eisendrath, Hannah	Chicago/IL
Eisendrath, Georges	Krasinem/Belgium
Eisendrath-Meert, Claudine	Krasinem/Belgium
Eisendrath, Henri	Brussels/Belgium
Segers, Maggy	Brussels/Belgium

Eisendrath, John	Los Angeles/CA
Levin, Jennifer	Los Angeles/CA
Eisendrath, Max	Los Angeles/CA
Eisendrath, Sam	Los Angeles/CA
Eisendrath, Ava	Los Angeles/CA
Eisendrath, Ben	Los Angeles/CA
Eisendrath, Mary	Richmond/VA
Eisendrath, Rachel K.	Washington D.C.
Eisendrath, Paul	Ekeren/Belgium
Eisendrath-Van Houtte, Michèle	Ekeren/Belgium
Eisendrath, Richard	Oceanside/CA
Eisendrath, Diane	Oceanside/CA
Eisendrath, John	Oceanside/CA
Eisendrath, Becky	Oceanside/CA
Eisendrath, Michael	Oceanside/CA
Eisendrath, Matthew	Oceanside/CA
Eisendrath, Stefan	Lennik/Belgium
Florence, Elisabeth Nathan	New Rochelle/NY
Florence, Jocelyn	New Rochelle/NY
Mossmann, Mary Richter	Wheaton/IL
Mossmann, Allen	Wheaton/IL
Silberstein, Edith	Hastings-on-Hudson, NY
Stern, Jeffrey Richard	Baltimore/Maryland
Stern, Richard Eisendrath	Wolla/CA

Authors

Aschoff, Diethard: Dr phil., Professor (retd.) at the University of Münster, Staff Member of Institutum Judaicum Delitzschianum, author of uncountable publications on Jewish and regional history

Brinkmann, Tobias: Dr phil., Malvin and Lea Bank Associate Professor of Jewish Studies and History, Penn State University/USA, research and publications on Jewish and migration history

Cosanne-Schulte-Huxel, Elisabeth: Member of the Museums Association Board, co-founder of the Jewish Museum of Westphalia, research and publications on the regional history of Jews in Westphalia

Drüing, Helmut: studied English and American literature & history and Catholic Theology in Münster/Westphalia. He is working in the agricultural business thus having a deep insight into the social life of the rural population. In 2001, he started a parallel career as a writer of "plattdeutsche" theatre plays which reflect these experiences in the beloved lower German dialect.

Eichmann, Johanna: former teacher and school director, member of the Ursuline congregation of Dorsten, co-founder and former director of the Jewish Museum of Westphalia, now Honorary President, publications on Jewish history and culture

Reichling, Norbert: Dr phil., Sociologist, Civic Education teacher, Chairman of the Museums Association "Verein für jüdische Geschichte und Religion", Director of the Jewish Museum of Westphalia, research and publications on Memorial Culture and Civic Education

Schaap, Erik: living and working in Zaandam, is a publisher. He wrote many articles and books about World War II and manages the website www.joodsmonumentzaanstreek.nl, which contains the stories of about five hundred Jewish people who lived in the Zaanstreek region during World War II.

Schiffer, Walter: M.A., M.Th., teacher at the Dorsten Grammar School St. Ursula, lecturer on Jewish traditions and philosophical questions

Seppi, Barbara: Employee of the City Marketing Office (stadinfo Dorsten) and journalist

Ulfkotte, Josef: Dr phil., teacher at the Dorsten Grammar School "Gymnasium Petrinum", researcher on local history

Thanks

Many people have contributed to the production of this documentation. My thanks go firstly to all the authors of this documentation who put a great deal of time and energy into the research of the talks and papers. I would also like to express my thanks to the museum team who, with their work and know-how, contributed to the idea of the family reunion and now the documentation: Dr. Norbert Reichling, Gisela Brückner, Dr. Bert Schreiber, Professor Dr. Werner Springer, Thomas Ridder M.A. and our Honorary President Sister Johanna Eichmann. Thank you for many years of constructive work together.

Many thanks to our professional translator team: Patricia van den Brink, Laurence Browning and Petra Schickedanz.

The pictures used for this publication have been contributed by Adam Eisendrath, Georges Eisendrath, Werner Hagedorn, Hedwig Hauptvogel, Anke Klapsing-Reich, Norbert Reichling, Holger Steffe and Christel Winkel – many thanks to them.

Sincere thanks also to our Eisendrath hosts: Dr. Mechthild and Dr. Bert Schreiber, Mechthild and Hans Lienemann, Sister Scholastika Kirschner (Ursuline Convent), Edda and Bernd Pontow, Elisabeth and Friedrich Schulte-Huxel, Paul Schulte-Huxel, Gabriele and Professor Dr. Werner Springer, Ellen and Dr. Peter Staden, Christel and Bernd Winkel, Angelika and Otto Zenge.

My special thanks go to the Mayor of Dorsten, Lambert Lütkenhorst, for his great commitment, to Hedwig and Heinz Hauptvogel for the entertaining evening in Marl, to Helmut Drüing for appearing as a "Kiäpenkiärl" – a pedlar – at the Heimathaus in Haltern-Lippramsdorf, to Professor Dr. Martin Korda for his excellent and friendly guided tour in Münster, to Barbara Seppi as Julia Eisendrath in Dorsten, to Dr. Reinildis Hartmann for the silk cloths and to Count Ferdinand von Merveldt for welcoming everybody to Lembeck Castle. But I also thank all the other unmentioned people for their hard work in helping to make the family reunion such a success.

I thank all the sponsors for their generous financial contributions and, last but not least, Charles Eisendrath for his generous donation on the occasion of his 70th birthday. Without his generosity the documentation would not have been possible in this form.

We thank all the members of the Eisendrath family. We were so happy to receive your good wishes, your kind words and the signs of close bonds with Dorsten. For us they are both the motivation and obligation to continue our work.

Thank you for all the kind words for my colleagues from the museum, for the friends and hosts in Dorsten, for the translators and for me.

The Jewish Museum of Westphalia (Dorsten)

In June 1992 the Jewish Museum of Westphalia started its first activities in Dorsten, a small town located in North Rhine-Westphalia. The Museum is a private institution run by the "Association for Jewish History and Religion" (Verein für jüdische Geschichte und Religion) and the "Jewish Museum of Westphalia Foundation". The museum's staff incorporates 3 employees and more than 30 volunteers. A modern extension was built and opened in 2001 –it is here that the permanent exhibition is now housed.

Visitors have the opportunity to experience Jewish history and culture in a regional context. The permanent exhibition covers the issues "Jewish Religion and Culture" and "Jews in Westphalia". The first part focuses on "Torah – Synagogue – Community", the subject of "Home – Family – Individual" as well as "Jewish Life in Westphalia – Destruction and a New Start". A photo section "New Jewish Life in Westphalia" gives some impressions of present Jewish community life. In the "Jewish lives in Westphalia" division, fourteen biographies illustrate the history of Jewish people women – merchants, teachers, artists, rabbis, politicians, footballers and others - in Westphalia from the Middle Ages to the present day.

Research and publications are in most cases devoted to regional questions. Special exhibitions on art, history and human rights issues are housed in the old building of the Museum. Lectures, workshops for young and adult visitors and concerts are offered constantly. A library with more than 6000 books on Jewish culture and history provides interested visitors with a wealth of information.